# Victorian Cross Stitch

# Victorian Cross Stitch

## Jane Greenoff

A DAVID & CHARLES CRAFT BOOK

*To Bill, who is still my*
*best friend in spite of this book*

*Photography by* Di Lewis

**British Library Cataloguing in Publication Data**
Greenoff, Jane
  Victorian cross stitch.
  1. Embroidery. Cross-stitch
  I. Title
  746.443

  ISBN 0-7153-9828-8

Typeset by ABM Typographics Limited, Hull
and printed in Italy
by OFSA S.p.A.
for David & Charles plc
Brunel House   Newton Abbot   Devon

*Distributed in the United States by
Sterling Publishing Co Inc
387 Park Avenue South New York NY 10016-8810

# Foreword

My first experience of Victorian needlework was an embroidered picture of luscious full-blown roses that had been stitched in cross stitch, with the addition of lovely shaded beads. When I was shown the hand-painted paper charts known as Berlin designs from which the designs had been taken, my addiction to Victorian embroidery, particularly Berlin work, was assured.

Most Berlin work was embroidered in cross stitch, although usually in wools and on canvas. I have always felt that the designs could be adapted for fine cross stitch on linen and early in 1990 I had my chance to experiment.

Due to a chance meeting, I had the opportunity to visit Germany and discuss Berlin work with an expert, Ursula Joka. Ursula had already experimented with old designs which she worked in her lovely Flower Thread and she allowed me to study her marvellous collection. The designs in this book are the result of that extraordinary and inspiring opportunity. I hope that cross stitch enthusiasts everywhere will find something special here and enjoy reading this book as much as I have enjoyed researching and writing it.

# Contents

# Introduction

*Will anyone, a hundred years from now, consent to live in the houses the Victorians built, travel by their roads and railways, value the furnishings they made to live among?*

H. G. WELLS (1911)

H. G. Wells would have been greatly surprised to see today's fascination with everything Victorian, but there is no doubt that Victorian style has had a lasting influence, and the field of embroidery is no exception. Cross stitch has never ceased to be popular and today is enjoying a revival of interest both in traditional and experimental embroidery.

Interest in embroidery in the nineteenth century began slowly, but captured the imagination of the fashionable upper and new middle classes who had increased leisure time and money to spend on the new Berlin charts and materials. As its name suggests, Berlin work was introduced from the German city of that name from the early 1800s, for although there had been charts for needlework for many years, the first documented coloured chart appeared in 1804. This type of embroidery acquired its name because Berlin wool was used to make the stitches, but the name Berlin work actually includes a much wider range of needlework than is apparent at first glance. As the popularity of counted needlework increased, many charts began to be printed in colour, although the more complex designs were always hand-painted. These hand-painted charts were interpreted using wool, silk, cotton and beads, and were worked on linen, gauze and canvas. The painted charts that were used as patterns for such embroidery are now very collectable and therefore expensive. The

*Victorian watercolour*

charts are works of art in their own right, and sadly rarely include the name of the artist. (The unknown artists were usually women, but only the names of the men who published the charts are recorded!)

All the designs in *Victorian Cross Stitch* are counted designs, so that once you have mastered the technique, it will be possible to stitch them all yourself. Cross stitch is not a Victorian stitch, however, for it was included in the earliest dated and signed English sampler in 1598. Jane Bostocke's sampler, which is now in the Victorian and Albert Museum, used cross stitch, French knots and back stitch as well as other counted stitches.

The term 'counted' means that the design is transferred on to the fabric by placing each stitch in the right place using the chart as the pattern. By definition it can be the most personal sort of needlework because although you follow a basic pattern, you are still creating the design on a blank piece of fabric. Counting the design on to the fabric is a completely different process from working a design with the pattern printed on to the fabric. There is a chance with some printed designs that if the printing is not very accurate the stitches may appear out of position and the results can be disappointing. However, once you have mastered the technique of counting you may never buy a printed design again!

Any form of needlework can develop into an absorbing hobby, but counted needlework has enormous scope because you, the stitcher, are in control. The fabric used for counted cross stitch is free of any printing or transfer, so you can develop your own ideas and patterns. If you do not like a design, or part of a design, you can simply alter it. As with any counted design, the patterns can be stitched on a suitable canvas in wools if desired.

As you collect charts, books and even kits, try to keep every scrap of thread and spare fabric, and before long you will be stitching designs with odds and ends. There is no satisfaction like giving a card for a special occasion which has been stitched using left-over materials. A small hand-stitched card is always a special gift.

Instructions for each project illustrated are included, although you will have to adapt some of the charts yourself – for example, the Beaded Lily Purse on p96. This design has been adapted from the chart for the Lily Tray on p78.

The stitch used in all the projects is cross stitch, but a few other counted stitches are included where pretty finishing techniques are needed. The fabrics used are all readily available even-weave materials – usually linen, Aida or Hardanger produced by Zweigart. The stranded cottons are all DMC, although the author's own exchange chart for German Flower Thread is included on p15. Further details about the materials used in the book are given in the next section.

Imperial measurements have been used throughout with metric measurements indicated in brackets.

# CHAPTER 1
# Materials and Equipment

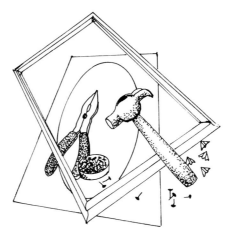

For any form of counted needlework you will need an even-weave fabric. This means that the weft (horizontal threads) and the warp (vertical threads) are woven evenly to give the same number of threads in each direction. As the designs are based on a square stitch, it is vital that the fabric has an even weave (see Fig 1). Although it would be possible to count accurately the threads on ordinary linen, your stitches could become squashed and the design distorted. Fabric choice is a matter of personal taste and your eyesight's limitations. The variety of fabrics on the market today means that everyone should be able to find something suitable for their embroidery. Specialist materials are also made that combine brocade or satin-type finishes with an even-weave fabric like Aida to give the cross stitcher even more choice.

When choosing materials for counted cross stitch, the 'thread count' is the method used by manufacturers to differentiate between the varieties available – for example, the more threads or stitches to the inch, the finer the fabric.

To start with, choose a fabric that you can see without too many artificial aids, as you can advance to finer, more delicate fabrics when you have mastered the counting technique. When buying your fabric, do check with the shop assistant that the material you have selected is suitable. If you buy a kit, choose a small one so that you can finish it reasonably quickly and check that the fabric in the packet is easy for you to work with. Some good shops will exchange the fabric if you feel that it is too fine for your requirements.

Although the projects in this book may be stitched on a variety of fabrics and materials, linen, Aida, Hardanger and Linda are ideal for perfecting your technique. And remember that any of the designs may be worked on any fabric as long as it is even weave.

*(overleaf) Assorted needlework materials*

11

## FABRIC

### LINEN

Although a good quality, even-weave linen is expensive, it is lovely to handle and lends itself to delicate cross stitch. Linen is made of natural fibres, so the thickness of the threads may vary slightly, which is why the technique for stitching on linen is different from that required for other even-weave materials. When using linen, the cross stitches are worked over two strands in each direction (see Fig 1), thus balancing any discrepancies.

Some projects in this book use an unbleached linen to achieve an 'antique' effect. The colour of these untreated linens does vary, so check that you like the colour and that your choice of coloured threads works on that particular shade.

*Fig 1 Cross stitch on linen*

### AIDA AND HARDANGER

These cotton fabrics have been specially produced for counted needlework. The two threads are woven in blocks rather than singly and a cross stitch is worked over a single block (see Fig 2). To begin with, you may find it easier to count using this type of fabric, but some of the projects do require the durability and softness of linen.

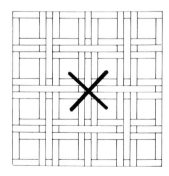

*Fig 2 Cross stitch on Aida*

### LINDA

This cotton fabric has a soft unglazed look which is ideal for table linen and napkins, as it washes well and is available in a variety of colours.

## PERFORATED PAPER

This specialist paper has been available for many years and is regaining popularity with stitchers. This excellent product can be stitched, folded, glued and cut to make a variety of lovely gifts and novelties. The Victorians were very fond of using perforated paper, both for stitching and paper sculpture. The art of perforated paper needlework enjoyed its heyday during the nineteenth century. European ladies would take classes in cutting and stitching techniques and some very elaborate designs were produced.

Victorian paper needlework was often in the form of bookmarks of a religious nature, with verses or pieces of scripture worked in cross stitch or long stitch. Some of the samplers seen in Victorian scenes would have been stitched on paper, later examples included needle- and card-cases, table-mats, lampshades and even handkerchief boxes.

Early examples of stitched paper are very collectable and prices have increased in recent years. Antique paper had more holes to the inch than the paper available today, so the scale of modern designs must be altered slightly to take this difference into account.

## THREADS

During the last decade the number of threads, both natural and synthetic, that are available for needlework has increased tenfold and it would be impossible to discuss them all here. A variety of materials has been used in the book and will be discussed later. The list that follows is a selection to whet your appetite.

### STRANDED COTTON (FLOSS)

This is probably the most commonly used embroidery thread and is generally available in one form or another. Where a stranded cotton has been used in the models photographed, the shade numbers referred to are DMC threads.

Stranded cotton is made up of six strands of mercerised cotton (this gives the thread its familiar sheen and finish). The thread can be split into the number of strands required as you stitch. Each design in the book will indicate how many strands to use, although you can always experiment with your own ideas. Care and management of threads and materials will be dealt with in a separate section.

*GERMAN FLOWER THREAD (JOKA-GARN)*
This soft unmercerised single-ply cotton thread with a fine matt finish is ideal for cross stitch. It has a wonderful colour range and is also colour-fast, making it ideal for table and bed linens.

*MARLITT THREAD*
This shiny Viscose thread has a strong gloss and usually comes in vibrant colours. It can be very effective when a striking contrast is required.

*DESIGNER SILK*
This comparatively new thread is a spun Chinese silk, which is dyed by hand with acid dyes. The Designer Silks used in the book are space dyed and blended throughout the spectrum, so that the colour changes are subtle and the lustre of the silk is used in the design.

*CHOOSING THREADS*
When selecting your threads, always have the fabric you are intending to use as a background with you, as it will affect your choice of colours. When you are in the shop, check the colour of the threads in daylight or, if possible, on a daylight box (a special light that does not affect the colour shades). Daylight bulbs are now available to fit both bayonet and screw fittings of domestic spotlights. The vast range of coloured threads that is available may seem overwhelming, but don't be daunted as similar shades blended together can be really effective. As you examine the charts in the book you will notice that the colours are often just a shade apart to add texture without too much contrast. After working a few designs, you will find that choosing your colours becomes easier and you will make fewer mistakes, so don't worry about any early mishaps.

*CARING FOR THREADS*
One of the most successful ways of keeping your threads in order while stitching is to use an organiser. Although organisers can be bought, you can just as easily make your own. You will need stiff card with punched holes down each side (see Fig 3) and a skein of stranded cotton. Cut the cotton into manageable lengths of about 20in

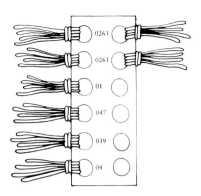

*Fig 3 An organiser*

(50cm), and thread them through the holes, labelled with their make and shade number. It is then easy to remove one length of thread without disturbing the rest. To divide the cotton, just split the number of threads you need and gradually pull apart. Don't jerk the threads as they tend to tangle. If you return the spare colours to the vacant hole opposite the shade number, it will prevent the threads from getting into a tangle. It also means that when the project is complete, you can keep the spare threads already marked with the shade number.

| THREAD EXCHANGE CHART | | | |
|---|---|---|---|
| German Flower Thread | DMC | German Flower Thread | DMC |
| 2061 | 677 | 2002 | 318 |
| 1049 | 972 | 3114 | 902 |
| 3001 | 367 | 2088 | 326 |
| 3403 | 334 | 2068 | 309 |
| 3822 | 336 | 1001 | – |
| 3702 | 500 | 1932 | 729 |
| 2000 | 3363 | 3412 | 975 |
| 3902 | 3345 | 1600 | 839 |
| 1500 | 613 | 3312 | 436 |
| 3512 | 640 | 3432 | 553 |
| 2001 | 320 | 1005 | 550 |
| 3832 | 700 | 1002 | 604 |
| 3101 | 704 | 3102 | 823 |
| 3732 | 3347 | 2115 | – |
| 3722 | 793 | 1350 | 958 |
| 3311 | 352 | 1009 | 561 |
| 1000 | ecru | 2079 | 321 |
| 2023 | 413 | 2041 | 3350 |
| 2099 | 368 | 2082 | 746 |
| 1003 | 961 | 3302 | 371 |

## BEADS

Most good needlework shops now keep a stock of suitable beads in a wide range of colours. Beads tend to lose their colour if they are kept in sunlight and the colour of some varieties will run.

## CHARTS

A needlework chart may be a series of symbols or coloured squares on graph paper (see Fig 4). The principle is the same for either type. Each square, both occupied and unoccupied, represents two threads of linen or one block of Aida. Each occupied square – ie, one that contains a symbol or colour – equals one stitch. At this stage each stitch is presumed to be a completed cross stitch, as other techniques will be explained later in the book. When using coloured charts, the designer will have shaded the chart to match as closely as possible the colour that has been used, but the chart itself is always limited to the available colouring materials and by the accuracy of colour reproduction. For this reason each chart in the book will include a key with appropriate reference numbers that relate to the worked model in the photographs. You will be able, of course, to use alternatives either from preference or because you have had difficulty in finding a particular product. In some cases the chart, or a part of it, can be used for more than one project, in which case advice on colour changes are included. Charts using symbols with a colour code may look complicated, but with practice you will be able to imagine the finished result. As you become experienced in the technique, you may wish to add or subtract colours to or from your designs, and you may even use additional materials. Designing and adapting charts is explained later.

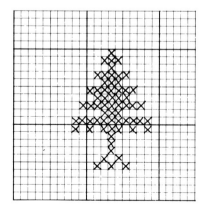

*Fig 4 A simple chart on graph paper*

## DESIGN SIZE

All that determines the size of a cross stitch design is the number of stitches up and down. If you are familiar with knitting, it is rather like wool and needle sizes. The same number of stitches worked in a fine 4-ply wool would give you a totally different look if it was worked in a chunky Aran-weight wool. The same design worked on fine silk gauze and on thick canvas using the same chart would give very different results.

To calculate the design size, look at the chart and count the stitches in each direction, ie the number of squares on the chart that are coloured or are occupied by a symbol. Test yourself by counting the squares on one of the charts in the chapter 'First Projects' and comparing the number with the given stitch count. Here's an example: 168 stitches (horizontal) × 140 stitches (vertical).

Next, check your chosen fabric to calculate how much you will need. You will need to know its thread count to estimate the completed dimensions: place a ruler on top of your fabric and, using a needle, count the number of threads or blocks to the inch. A cross stitch is worked over two threads in each direction when using linen and one block if using Aida. Therefore, if the linen has 28 threads to the inch, there will be 14 stitches to the inch and so on. Using our stitch count example of 168 stitches × 140 stitches, the calculation is as follows:

168 @ 14 stitches to the inch = 12in
(horizontal finished size)
140 @ 14 stitches to the inch = 10in
(vertical finished size)

When the thread count of the fabric changes so will the finished size of the design. The following table shows how much the finished size of our example would vary with different fabrics.

| Fabric/Thread count (per inch) | Stitch count (per inch) | Finished size |
| --- | --- | --- |
| Linen/28 threads | 14 | 12 × 10in |
| Linen/30 threads | 15 | 11¼ × 8in |
| Aida/14 [blocks] | 14 | 12 × 10in |
| Aida/18 [blocks] | 18 | 9⅓ × 7¾in |

The crucial factor with any counted needlework is the number of stitches in the design; this and the thread count of the fabric will determine the size of the completed project. Remember, if you use a different fabric from the one shown in your chosen project, the finished size will be different.

Once you have calculated your design size you can decide how much fabric to buy. It is vital to allow a reasonable border for stretching and framing. About 3in (8cm) all the way round is a good guideline, although obviously if you are working a tiny design on linen, less would be appropriate. Some projects in the book are completed as books or bags rather than as pictures, so always check the size of the fabric required. Some shops will sell linen and Aida in pieces, but it is more usual to buy the length you require from a roll, which involves buying the fabric width as well. This will give you sufficient material to work a number of projects or possibly to share it with a friend. Once you have purchased your fabric, keep it wrapped to protect it from damage.

## FRAMES

Whether or not you use a frame is a matter of personal preference, although some designs are easier to manage on some form of frame or hoop.

Various sizes of hoops are available and these can be very helpful when you are stitching a small design. A hoop should only be used if the whole design will fit inside because moving the hoop can distort the fabric and your carefully sewn stiches. Some shops now stock attractive and inexpensive hoops that can be used to frame the completed project as well as for use while stitching.

Rectangular frames also come in a variety of

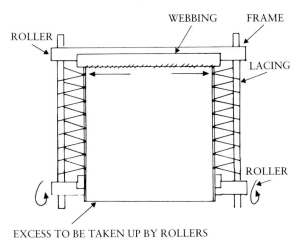

EXCESS TO BE TAKEN UP BY ROLLERS

*Fig 5 A needlework frame*

sizes and styles, some with floor or table stands to enable you to keep both your hands free. The needlework is stitched to the webbing along the width of the frame and the excess fabric is held on the rollers at the top and bottom (see Fig 5).

Upholstered frames can be made for the real enthusiast as the needlework is then pinned to the wadding and can be removed easily.

You may find that you work faster without a frame, but care must be taken to keep the tension even and neither too tight nor too slack.

## SCISSORS

You will need a sharp pair of dressmaking scissors for cutting your fabric. When cutting linen or Aida it is important to follow the line of threads to ensure that you have a straight edge. To check that the fabric is straight, pull out a thread at the edge, then trim to match if necessary. A small pair of pointed embroidery scissors are an essential accessory for the stitcher for trimming the ends of threads and for unpicking when all else fails. A scissor keeper (like a weighted pin-cushion) tied to the scissors will make them easy to find while you are working.

## NEEDLES

With all counted needlework you will need ball-point or blunt tapestry needles which will vary in size according to the fabric and the thread in use. The needle should slip through the fabric without enlarging the hole, but should not fall through without a little pressure.

Avoid leaving the needle in the fabric when you put it away, as needles can mark the fabric and even go rusty. On some designs, especially those that involve a coloured border, you may find that it is helpful to thread a number of needles with different colours to save changing needles every few stitches.

Some stitchers find that their needles mark and discolour very quickly and that they need to re-place them at regular intervals. The only answer is to treat yourself to a gold-plated tapestry needle.

Some projects include small beads in the design; beading needles are available, but the beads can be stitched easily using a fine 'sharp' needle and a half cross stitch.

# CHAPTER 2

# Cross Stitch Explained

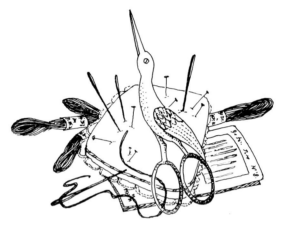

## STARTING OFF

As in all forms of needlework, using a knot to anchor the first stitch is frowned upon, unless you are planning to cut it off once the work is started. This is not just the purist view. A knot causes an unsightly mass at the back of your work, it can pull through to the right side when the work is stretched, and it gets in the way of later work. The appearance of the back of the work is particularly important on table linens or bookmarks.

### KNOTS ON THE RIGHT SIDE

After threading your needle (do use one of the excellent needle-threaders which reduce frustration) and knotting the end, pierce the fabric on the right side away from your intended stitch. Bring the needle up where you intend to start your first cross and work three or four stitches towards the knot, thus anchoring the thread. Push the needle to the back of the work and, checking that the thread is anchored, snip off the excess thread and the knot from the front. Avoid using this method with very dark colours, particularly black, as they can leave small marks or 'shadows' which are

difficult to remove (a small clean toothbrush is very useful for removing unwanted 'whiskers').

### KNOT ON THE WRONG SIDE

Bring the needle up where you intend to start, feeling the knot with the other hand and leaving about 1in (2.5cm) of thread. Work a few stitches, then return to the wrong side, anchor the thread and snip off the extra thread and the knot.

### KNOTLESS LOOP START

This method can be very useful with stranded cotton, but it doesn't work unless you intend to stitch with two strands. Cut the stranded cotton to roughly twice the length that you would usually sew with, and carefully separate one strand. Double this thread and thread your needle. Pierce your fabric from the wrong side where you intend to start your first stitch, leaving the looped end at the rear of the work (see Fig 6). Return your needle to the wrong side after forming a half cross stitch and pass the needle through the waiting

*An original Berlin chart*

18

*Fig 6 Knotless loop start*

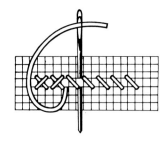

*Fig 7b Cross stitch in two journeys*

loop. Thus the stitch is anchored and the work can continue. This method is unsuitable for threads with a nap or 'direction' (wool or flower thread), as you will have threads facing different directions.

## WORKING THE STITCH

For this example the stitch is being worked on linen, over two threads of the fabric with two strands of stranded cotton.

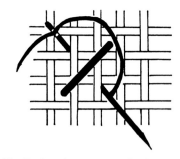

*Fig 7a Single cross stitch showing needle position*

Bring the needle up through the wrong side at the bottom left and cross two fabric threads and insert at the top right. To do this, either count two up and two along or vice versa. Push the needle through and bring up at the bottom right-hand corner, ready to complete the cross stitch in the top left corner (see Fig 7a). To work the adjacent cross, bring the needle up at the bottom right-hand corner of the first stitch; thus the stitches share points on entry and exit. Each first half must always slant the same way, to give your stitches a regular appearance and sheen.

For an alternative method, work the first half of the stitch but instead of completing the stitch, work the next half stitch and continue to the end of the row. The crosses are completed on the return journey. (see Fig 7b)

## PRACTICE PIECE

Using a small piece of fabric, work the little test design shown in Fig 4. Depending on your fabric, experiment with the number of strands in your needle, so that the fabric is covered, but remember that some holes will be occupied by part of four cross stitches and that you don't want to distort the fabric. If you are stitching on linen and you are not sure of the number of threads needed, the best way is to pull out carefully a thread of the fabric and compare this with your chosen yarn. The thread on your needle should be roughly the same weight as that of the fabric unless you are planning to add texture intentionally (see knot Garden Flower Press, p123). Other counted stitches are used in the book and will be explained in the relevant chapters, although all the same basic rules apply.

## STITCHING A DESIGN

At last you are ready to start and you are faced with a plain piece of fabric and a chart with a design on it. If you follow the instructions below you will see how simple it is:

1. Lightly press your fabric and fold it into four.
2. Open out and stitch a line of tacking stitches along the creases following the threads (see Fig 8).
3. Check that you have all the colours you need (to make an organiser, see Fig 3).
4. Mount all the threads on a card alongside the shade number (see Fig 3).
5. Sew a narrow hem or oversew to prevent fraying. This can be removed on completion (see Fig 8).
6. Thread your needle with the required number of threads and you are ready to start.

Generally, you will begin in the middle of the fabric and proceed outwards towards the border.

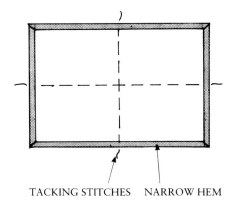

TACKING STITCHES    NARROW HEM

*Fig 8 A narrow hem and lines of tacking stitches*

This is good advice, particularly for beginners. Even experienced stitchers can run out of fabric, having guessed their starting point. Look at your chart. Find the middle and check which colour is used. Thread your needle and place the first cross stitch on the fabric where the lines of tacking threads cross.

At this point you have to decide in which direction to work. It is probably the best policy to work towards smallish gaps, as counting over large areas of blank fabric can be nerve-racking. Remember that you are counting the threads and not the spaces. Ginnie Thompson (one of the best cross stitch teachers) always says, 'Think of it as a ladder and count the rungs, not the holes'. When you do have a large gap to cross, do not carry the thread, unless it can be carried behind existing stitches. Threads left behind the open weave of the fabric will show on the right side. You will no doubt develop techniques of your own, but below are some tried and tested hints.

GOLDEN RULES
1 Always work with clean hands.
2 Do not work in a fluffy woollen jumper
3 Keep the work wrapped when it is not in use (pillow-cases take an average size frame easily).
4 Mount colours on an organiser and identify with the make and shade number.
5 Check that you have enough thread to finish the project as dye lots vary.
6 Sew a hem around the fabric to prevent fraying.
7 Don't use knots to anchor the stitches.
8 Work from the centre to ensure an adequate border for stretching and framing.
9 Don't travel between areas of colour unless the thread can be hidden behind existing stitches.
10 Never have coffee or other drinks near your work.
11 Finish off the ends as you go – don't leave them all to the end.
12 The cross stitches should all be worked in the same direction, with the first half starting the same way every time.

## GUIDELINES FOR STITCHING ON PAPER
Using paper for embroidery is not new, but it has only recently been readily available. My nine-year-old son and his friends have made some lovely gifts using cross stitch and paper, so it is ideal for beginners. Here are some helpful hints:

1 Although the paper is quite strong, do remember to handle it with care because it will tear if it is handled roughly.
2 There is a right and a wrong side to the paper, the smoother side being the right side.
3 Avoid folding the paper unless this is part of the design. Find the centre with a ruler and mark with a pencil. The lines can be removed with a soft rubber.
4 Use three strands for the cross stitch and two strands for any back stitch outlining.
5 Keep the paper flat while stitching and cut out when the work is complete, following the cutting lines on the chart.

## PRESSING CROSS STITCH
If you do not want to flatten your embroidery, the secret of success is not the iron, although it must be absolutely clean, but the surface used for ironing. Cover the ironing-board with a clean, white, soft towel. When the cross stitch is placed on the covered board, face down on the towel, the action of pressing with the iron actually helps the cross stitch to stand above the fabric. It has almost an embossed look when pressed properly. A steam iron or a dry iron and a damp cloth work perfectly well if there is a soft surface underneath.

## STRETCHING AND MOUNTING
The following important rules should be adhered to when stretching and framing a piece of needle-

work to prevent spoiling all your hard work:

1 When mounting a piece of embroidery, always use acid-free paper or card (available from good stationery or art shops) to prevent long-term damage to the fabric.
2 Use natural threads – ie cotton or linen for any stitching necessary.
3 Do not over-stretch the needlework, but cut the mount board the right size.
4 Always have sufficient space between the glass and the needlework so that the embroidery is not in contact with the glass.

*MOUNTING NEEDLEWORK*

To make up your design as a picture, it is worth the time and effort to mount the piece yourself rather than to send the work to a framer. It will be much cheaper and really doesn't take long once you have mastered the technique. You can either use acid-free mount card or cover other card with acid-free paper. Light-weight foam board is now available which is ideal for mounting cross stitch. It is also possible to cover a piece of card with a natural fabric (cotton, ideally) and this can be fixed with a rubber-based adhesive and left to dry.

When mounting the small novelty projects, you may manage the whole procedure with some double-sided sticky tape, but it is worth taking the time and trouble with larger projects.

There are two basic methods of attaching the worked piece to the mount board:

1 Pin the work to the edge of the board and stitch in place (see Figs 9 and 10).
2 Pin the work to the board and lace across the back using strong linen thread (see Fig 11).

When you pin a piece of linen or Aida to the edge of your covered mount board, it must be centred and stretched evenly, ensuring that all the margins are the same (it is customary to leave a slightly larger border at the bottom of a picture). Once the board is cut to size and prepared for mounting, measure across the bottom edge and mark the centre with a glass-headed pin. Take the worked piece of needlework and mark the centre stitch along the bottom with a pin and match these up to ensure that the fabric is in the right place. Working out from the centre of each edge, pin through the fabric following a line of threads until all four sides are complete.

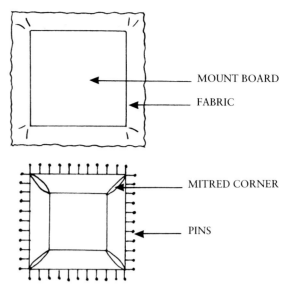

*Fig 9 Pinning the material along the edge of the card*

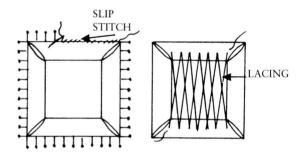

*Figs 10/11 Stitching the fabric along the edge and lacing the excess material*

If you use method 1, stitch through the needlework and the fabric, covering the board using the strong thread (of natural origin) and removing the pins as you go.

If you use method 2, the spare fabric is laced across the back of the board, two sides at a time.

Whichever method you prefer, always work on clean surfaces and with clean hands. This is particularly relevant in hot weather when your hands perspire.

## WASHING NEEDLEWORK

Avoid washing embroidery as threads are not always colour-fast. If it is necessary, handwash with great care in lukewarm water and soap flakes. Tenestar, which contains no bleach, is also recommended for silk yarns.

# CHAPTER 3

# Simple Projects

These pretty projects are designed to help you master the techniques of counted cross stitch, with a few hints to make the whole process as painless as possible. The four projects in this chapter are all bookmark shape, although you will see that one of the designs has been made up as a door-plate. In Chapter 6 there is a Victorian tidy which uses one of the small flower motifs from the door-plate, and in Chapter 12 there is a book made from a simple repeating pattern which would make a lovely bookmark or door-plate. You can alter and adapt designs as you wish.

# OUR FATHER

This simple bookmark is stitched on a purchased 'embroidery band', but it could be worked on any even-weave material.

*Stitch count:* 70 × 18
*Design size:* 5 × 1⅓in (12.5 × 3cm)

MATERIALS *(See chart, p26)*
*Embroidery band in 'antique' colour: 28 threads to 1in (12 threads to 1cm)*
*Stranded cottons 936, 470 and black — two strands for the cross stitch, one for the outline*
*Marlitt Viscose threads 819, 857 and 1013 — two strands for both the cross stitch and the outline*
*Purchased tassel*

Refer to the Golden Rules on p21. If you are using a ready hemmed embroidery band, you can go to the next paragraph. If not, sew a narrow hem around the material to prevent fraying.

Lightly press the fabric, fold in four, and stitch the tacking lines as described on p20. Look at the chart and find the centre of the design. In this case the centre is in the middle of the back stitch writ-

ing (see colour chart). It is probably easier to work some cross stitch to start with, so begin the design by placing the needle at the point where your tacking lines cross and count down from there. The twelfth square down from your middle point is a deep purple stitch. Thread your needle with two strands of the Marlitt thread and work four cross stitches as shown on the chart.

Following the colour chart (graph), gradually build up the design, working the main flower and adding the leaves and detail as you go. The outline to the flower and leaves is worked in back stitch using one strand of dark green (936) when the cross stitch is worked. Always add the outline after the cross stitch to keep the lines crisp and unbroken. The writing is also worked in back stitch, but using two strands of black stranded cotton.

When the stitching is complete, check for any missed stitches and press the embroidery on the wrong side, (see p21).

In the example illustrated, the bookmark is completed by fraying the top edge of the material and trimming the bottom margin with a purchased tassel. To fray the top edge, see the next project.

23

# THE HOLY BIBLE

This bookmark is stitched on a specialist embroidery material with a ready-made ornamental edge. If you are unable to find this type of fabric, work the design on linen or Aida and hem stitch the edge as shown on p46.

*Stitch count:* 14 × 78
*Design size:* 1 × 5½in (2.5 × 14cm)

*MATERIALS (See chart, p29)*
*Embroidery band in ivory fabric: 30 threads to 1in (13 threads to 1cm)*
*Marlitt Viscose threads as shown on chart: use two strands for the cross stitch and one strand for the back stitch*

Work a narrow hem around the fabric unless you are using an embroidery band, in which case you can start stitching straight away.

Work the design as explained in the instructions for the Our Father bookmark, using the chart as the pattern. Marlitt thread has a lovely sheen to it, but does tend to be a little difficult to control. It seems to have a mind of its own, so treat it firmly. This design could also be stitched in stranded cotton or Flower Thread (see Thread Exchange Chart, p15). When the cross stitch is complete, the flowers are outlined in one strand of ruby (1209) using a small back stitch (see Fig 12). The writing is also stitched in back stitch but uses two strands to give it more impact.

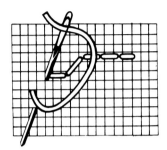

*Fig 12 Back stitch*

When the writing and outline are complete, check for missed stitches and lightly press the embroidery on the wrong side.

The example in the picture is shown with a frayed edge, although the design could be completed by hem stitching or trimming with ribbons. To add a frayed edge, decide how much border you need around the stitching, and, using a toning thread, work a line of back stitch across the top and bottom of the design, fray the edge to the back stitch and trim the ends to neaten.

*Bible bookmarks: Our Father, and The Holy Bible*

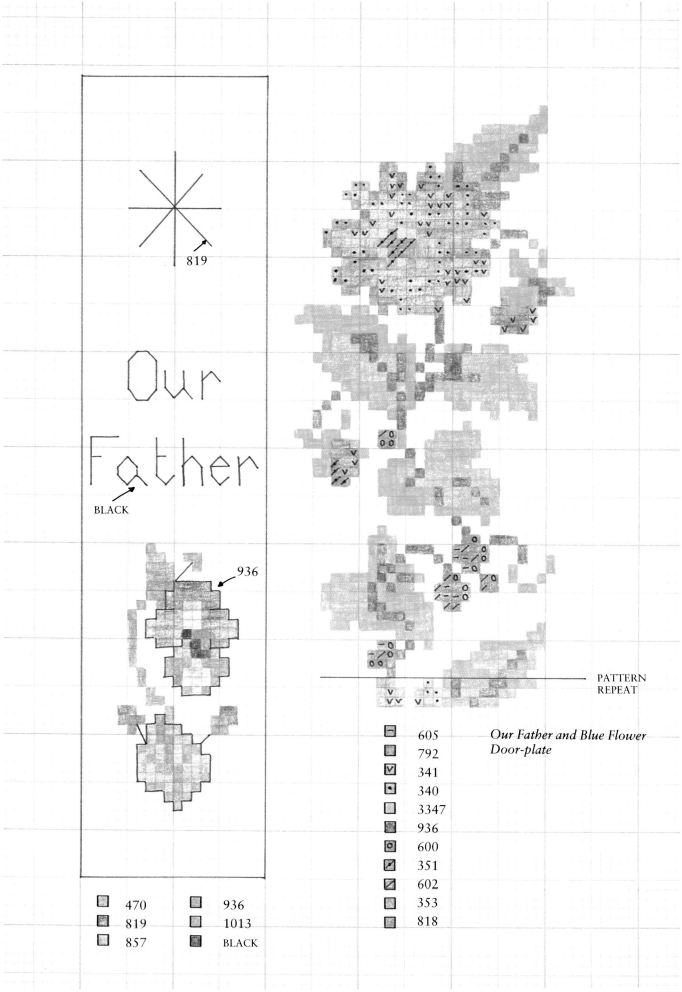

819

Our Father

BLACK

936

PATTERN REPEAT

| | | |
|---|---|---|
| ⊟ | 605 | |
| ▣ | 792 | |
| ☑ | 341 | *Our Father and Blue Flower* |
| ▪ | 340 | *Door-plate* |
| ▢ | 3347 | |
| ▨ | 936 | |
| ◉ | 600 | |
| ◪ | 351 | |
| ◪ | 602 | |
| ▣ | 353 | |
| ▣ | 818 | |

| | | | | |
|---|---|---|---|---|
| ▣ | 470 | ▣ | 936 | |
| ▣ | 819 | ▣ | 1013 | |
| ▣ | 857 | ▣ | BLACK | |

# HOME SWEET HOME

This little terrace of houses (overleaf) has been stitched on perforated paper to make a book-mark, although it would be possible to work the design on any even-weave material.

*Stitch count: 84 × 28*
*Design size: 6 × 2in (15 × 5cm)*

*MATERIALS (See chart, p29)*
*Perforated paper in cream: 14 holes to 1in (6 holes to 1cm)*
*Black perforated paper to mount design*
*Stranded cottons as shown on the colour chart*

If you wish to stitch this project on material, follow the instructions for either of the other bookmarks in this chapter. If you are working on paper, use the colour chart as the pattern and work the design from the middle, using three strands of stranded cotton for the cross stitch and two strands for the outlining. You will see from the colour picture and the chart that the roofs of the houses are worked in a mixture of threads to add texture and variety. To do this, simply mix the colours on your needle. If you look at the colour key to the terrace chart, you will see that two of the colours are shown with two shade numbers. Use one strand of the first shade and two strands of the second.

When the cross stitch is complete, add the back stitch outline using two strands of stranded cotton, check for missed stitches and cut out following the cutting lines on the chart. Mount onto black paper with double-sided sticky tape.

# BLUE FLOWER DOOR-PLATE

This lovely repeating pattern from an old Berlin chart is stitched on Aida and fitted into a purchased perspex door-plate (finger-plate).

*Stitch count: 142 × 29*
*Design size: 8 × 1¾in (20 × 4.5cm)*
*Door-plate dimensions: 10 x 2¼in (25 × 5.5cm)*

*MATERIALS (See chart opposite)*
*Aida fabric: 18 blocks to 1in (8 blocks to 1cm)*
*Perspex door-plate (finger-plate)*
*Stranded cottons as colour chart*
*Thin cardboard (cereal packet thickness is ideal)*

Cut a piece of Aida fabric at least 2in (5cm) larger than the door-plate – ie, allowing 1in (2.5cm) all the way round – and sew a narrow hem around the edge to prevent fraying. Lightly press the material in four and mark the creases with a line of tacking threads (see Fig 8).

Find the centre of the chart and thread your needle with one strand of stranded cotton. Using the colour chart as a guide, work the design from the centre, repeating the pattern until the embroidery fits your requirements.

When complete, check for missed stitches and press lightly with a damp cloth.

The embroidery will need to be mounted on to a piece of thin card before it is fitted into the door-plate. Cut a piece of card to fit inside the rim of the perspex, allowing just a little gap to accommodate the fabric. Centre the design under the perspex, and stretch the material over the card, folding the excess fabric underneath. Once the door-plate is screwed into place, the embroidery will remain in position.

*Home Sweet Home and Blue Flower Door-plate*

# Home Sweet Home and The Holy Bible

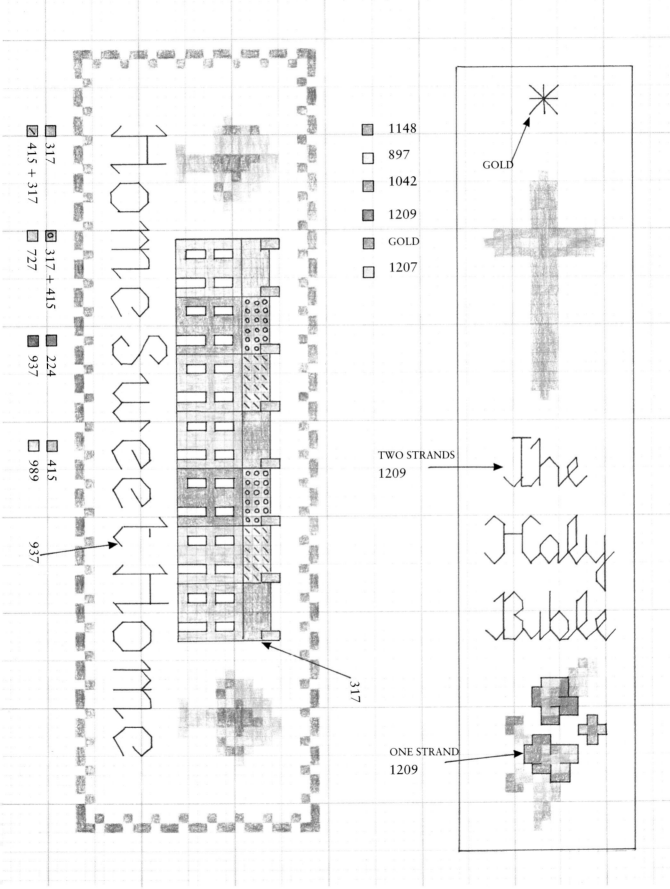

317

415 + 317

317 + 415
727

224
937

415
989

937

317

1148

897

1042

1209

GOLD

1207

GOLD

TWO STRANDS
1209

ONE STRAND
1209

# CHAPTER 4

# *Violets and Roses*

This beautiful alphabet sampler (p33) is one of my favourite projects. The idea was born about five years ago when I discovered a French sampler in a local antique shop. The exquisite design had been stitched by a child of eight using cross stitch, tent stitch and a few French knots. Each letter of the alphabet was worked in one colour and then decorated with a small flower. At the bottom, a vase of flowers finished it off perfectly.

The design illustrated adapts the decorated initials for use on more than just the picture. You will need to adapt the charts for your own use unless your initials happen to be 'J.G.'. If you enjoy cross stitch it would be worth investing in a pad of graph paper for designing and for layout plans. All you need is a pad of squared paper, ideally with the squares in blocks of ten – it makes adding up the stitches much easier.

The sampler is stitched on linen in cross stitch with a little back stitch outlining. You will see on the chart that the letters are shown outlined with one strand of green. This is optional – in fact, the letters are not outlined in the worked example in the colour picture. You may find that you need to add the back stitch if you are using the letters for a card or if you are stitching on a different fabric.

The needlecase and pin-cushion are stitched on linen using cross stitch for the letters, but the flower is worked using small glass beads. The simple sprigs of flowers on these two designs are adapted from the Roses Evening Bag in Chapter 10, using the chart on p92. The pin-cushion and needlecase each include some four-sided stitching to give a soft lacy effect. The pin-cushion has counted 'chain' stitch around the edge and the needlecase has a shaped edge finished with button-hole stitch.

The small oval brooch was stitched on black linen and completed with a purchased brooch fitting.

# VIOLET AND ROSE
# ALPHABET SAMPLER

The chart for this design has been divided in two to fit it on the page. The alphabet is charted on two pages with the mixed posy and a single rose on a separate chart.

*Stitch count:* 119 × 167 (the count shown is that of the completed stitched design)
*Design size:* 11½ × 7¾in (29 × 20cm), (as seen in colour picture)

*MATERIALS (See charts, pp34-6)*
*Linen in cream: 30 threads to 1in (13 threads to 1cm)*
*Stranded cottons as listed on the chart*

To work the alphabet sampler as illustrated, cut a piece of cream linen (check the thread count) at least 20 × 16in (51 × 41cm) to allow for the border and margin for stretching and framing.

Lay the design out on a large sheet of graph paper. Copy the outline of the letter 'S' in the centre of the paper and add the letters on either side, leaving a gap of three squares between each one. The letters above and below should be added, this time leaving a gap of five squares between the lines.

The design may be stitched from the colour chart, but using your layout plan to space the letters.

The single rose lies in the natural gap, top left, above the letter 'D' and the mixed posy fits below the letter 'T' in the bottom right of the picture.

The design should be stitched from the middle using two strands of stranded cotton for the cross stitch and one strand for any back stitch outline.

When the embroidery is complete, check for missed stitches and press on the wrong side. The finished piece may be framed as desired.

# BEADED PIN-CUSHION

*Stitch count:* 90 × 70
*Design size:* 6 × 4½in (15 × 11cm)

*MATERIALS (See charts, pp34-6, 92)*
*White linen: 30 threads to 1in (13 threads to 1cm)*
*Stranded cottons*
*Small glass beads (see below for number and colours)*
*Polyester toy filling (flame-retardant)*
*White linen thread*

Cut a piece of linen 9 × 7in (23 × 18cm), fold in four and press lightly. Sew a narrow hem around the edge to prevent fraying and stitch a line of

tacking threads along the folds to mark the centre lines.

The picture on p38 illustrates the position of the two initials and the relationship with the sprigs of blossom and the lines of four-sided stitch. To position the letters, carefully copy the letters onto graph paper, allowing three squares between them. The two sprigs of blossom are taken from the Roses Evening Bag chart on p92. One twig is taken directly from the chart and the other is turned upside down. Sketch their position on the graph paper, but work from the colour charts. In the example shown in the picture, the letters were stitched in green (DMC 562) and the area intended for the flower was covered in beads.

Choose beads that look the same shape and are the same size as the cross stitch. Each flower used three shades of pink or purple respectively and 45-50 beads. Each bead is positioned individually and stitched using half a cross stitch and a 'sharp' or beading needle.

When the cross stitch and beading are complete, the four-sided stitch is added to 'frame' the design. To ensure that the border of four-sided stitch is positioned correctly and does actually meet where it should, sew a line of small running stitches around the design, counting and stitching in groups of four threads (see Fig 13). The example illustrated has one row of four-sided stitch worked around the pattern.

### FOUR-SIDED STITCH

This very pretty stitch is simple to do and may be used for edges, folds and as a textured pattern. The idea is to stitch straight stitches on the front of the fabric, which, as you work, is pulled tight to form small holes or eyelets. The stitch is often worked in a matching thread as it is the effect on the fabric rather than the stitch itself that is so attractive. The thread will need to be pulled very tight, so a linen thread would be suitable.

The easiest way to understand four-sided stitch is to try it following the diagrams. The secret is to have straight stitches on the front and diagonal stitches on the back. No threads are removed for this stitch, so feel free to experiment.

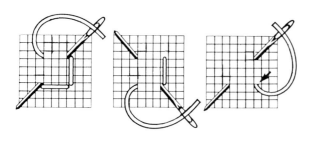

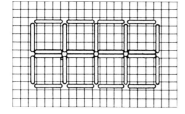

*Fig 13 Four-sided stitch*

The pin-cushion may be made up in a variety of ways. The worked piece in the picture has a row of chain stitch around the outer edge to disguise the seam. It is possible to work another row of chain stitch on the underneath section and once the two pieces have been sewn together, the rows of chain stitch can be 'whipped' with the same or contrasting colour to hide the join completely.

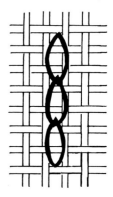

*Fig 14 Chain stitch*

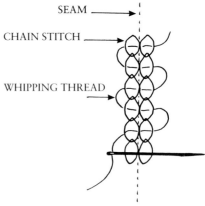

*Fig 15 Chain stitch with whipping*

Press the sections of the pin-cushion lightly with a damp cloth and check for missed stitches. Lay the embroidered material face up on a clean dry surface. Place the underneath section on top and carefully pin in position, making sure that the chain stitch has not become caught. Join the pieces together with small back stitches, leaving a small opening. Turn the work to the right side, press with a warm iron and stuff. You will be surprised at how much stuffing is needed to give a smooth and firm appearance. Ribbons or tassels may be added to the corners if wished.

*Violet and Rose Alphabet Sampler*

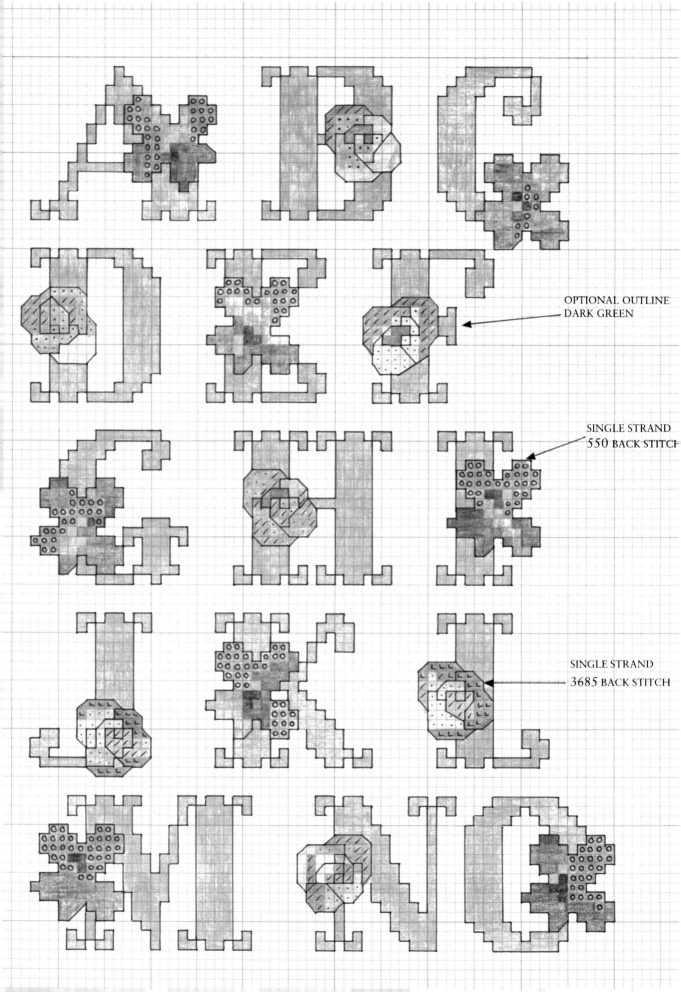

OPTIONAL OUTLINE
DARK GREEN

SINGLE STRAND
550 BACK STITCH

SINGLE STRAND
3685 BACK STITCH

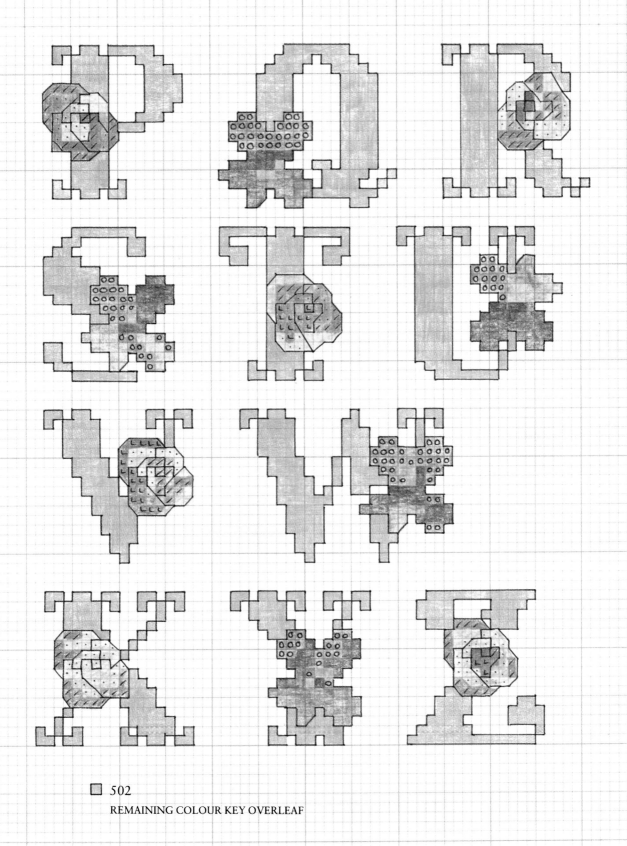

502

REMAINING COLOUR KEY OVERLEAF

*Violet and Rose Alphabet Sampler*

*Violet and Rose Alphabet Sampler*

| | |
|---|---|
| ☐ | 727 |
| ▨ | 470 |
| ▨ | 988 |
| ⊠ | 937 |
| ☐ | 772 |
| ▨ | 3885 |
| ◪ | 223 |
| ⊡ | 224 |
| ☐ | 818 |
| Ⓛ | 3350 |
| ⊙ | 327 |
| ▨ | 550 |
| ☐ | 554 |
| ▧ | BLACK |

# NEDLECASE

*Stitch count:* 42 × 55
*Design size:* 4 × 4½in (10 × 12cm) (size from spine to shaped edge)

MATERIALS *(See charts, pp34-6, 92)*
*White linen: 30 threads to 1in (13 threads to 1cm)*
*Medium-weight iron-on Vilene (interfacing)*
*Linen, flannel or felt for the 'pages'*
*Small glass beads*

Cut a piece of linen at least 12 × 6in (30 × 15cm) and fold in half, widthways, to make the front and back of the needlecase. The design will be worked on one half, the other piece becoming the back of the case. Sew two lines of tacking threads on the front section to enable you to centre the design.

TACKING THREADS

POSITION OF
BUTTON HOLE STITCH

BACK
SECTION

CENTRE OF
STITCHING

*Fig 16 The position of the tacking on
the needlecase*

Following the instructions for the pin-cushion in the previous section, trace the required initials onto graph paper, but one above the other. The sprig of blossom is the same motif as the pin-cushion, except that it curves above the letters. Work the initials as described in the previous section, adding the beads in the same fashion. The four-sided stitch is worked in two rows in a verti-

cal line up the middle of the needlecase to act as a sort of spine.

When the stitching is complete, check for missed stitches and press with a damp cloth.

Cut two pieces of Vilene the same size as the two sides of the needlecase and carefully pin them to the wrong side, folding in a small seam allowance along the line of four-sided stitches and hemming invisibly. Tack the rest of the lining in position, using plenty of stitches so that the materials don't 'creep' when the edge is button-holed.

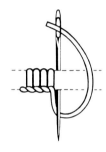

*Fig 17 Button-hole stitch*

Fold the needlecase along the spine and press lightly in the folded position. The easiest way to shape the edge is to sew a line of tacking threads in the form of a curve, checking the shape as you stitch. Once you are satisfied with the shape of the outline, work two more rows of stitches next to the first. This gives a line to follow when you add the button-hole stitch and helps to stay the curved edge as you stitch. Repeat this on the back of the needlecase, carefully matching the shape. The button-hole stitch is worked as shown using matching linen or button thread and stitching through all the layers of material. The edge is stitched before the fabric is cut, so don't panic! Use very sharp scissors when you cut the material and try to make clean cuts each time, as it is always much harder to tidy the edges afterwards.

Cut the pages the same shape as the needlecase and tie in position with matching ribbon.

*Needlecase, pin-cushion and oval brooch*

# OVAL BROOCH

*Design size:* 1½in (4cm) diameter

MATERIALS *(See charts, pp34-6)*

*Linen in black: 30 threads to 1in (13 threads to 1cm)*

*Purchased brooch*

Choose the initial and check the design size in the fabric you intend to use. Make sure it will fit your brooch fitting.

Stitch the design from the chart, check for missed stitches and press lightly on the wrong side. Make the brooch according to the manufacturer's instructions.

# CHAPTER 5

# *Verses in Stitches*

This chapter was inspired by the poem 'To a Daisy' by the Victorian poet James Montgomery. This delightfully simple poem seems to echo my own feelings about my much neglected garden. Thank goodness for daisies which will bloom and delight even when they are left untended. The design for the clock face is adapted from the daisy poem and again for the napkin. The design for the handkerchief case was originally intended for a bedroom cushion, but evolved a little differently. With the addition of some cream satin ribbon and two embroidered hankies, it makes a perfect present.

# SUMMER DAISY CLOCK

*Stitch count:* 88 × 95
*Design size:* 5 × 5½in (12.5 × 14cm)

*MATERIALS (See chart, p43)*
*Aida fabric in cream: 18 blocks to 1in (8 blocks to 1cm)*
*Stranded cottons as listed on the chart*
*Purchased acetate clock kit*

Cut a piece of Aida at least 7 × 9in (17.5 × 23cm), fold in four, sew a line of tacking threads along the folds to mark the centre, and work a narrow hem around the material to prevent fraying.

These instructions are guidelines only because the method will greatly depend on the chosen clock kit. A variety of kits are available, both in wooden cases and in the 'see-through' type illustrated. The clock was stitched as follows.

Remove the clock kit from its packaging and put the 'works' and the hands in a safe place. Place the Aida fabric on a clean dry surface and lay the clock face down on the material, matching the hole for the hands with the point where the tack-

ing lines cross, and the sides of the clock with the straight grain of the fabric. Draw around the clock with a soft tailor's pencil or chalk. The design must stay within this outline.

The numerals are the most important feature of the finished piece and if they are out of position the design will never look right. If the numbers are in the right place, the flowers or other decoration may be off-centre without any ill effects.

Work the clock from the chart using one strand of stranded cotton for both the cross stitch and the back stitch outline. The numbers are stitched in back stitch in one strand of dark green and the flowers are outlined in medium green. When complete, check for missed stitches and press lightly on the wrong side.

The worked clock in the picture was purchased complete with a self-adhesive, shaped mount board in the pack. A small hole was made at the central point and the needlework was stretched, mounted and the design squeezed between two layers of acetate. The 'works' and hands were added once the design was in position.

# TO A DAISY

Any favourite poem or piece of prose can be stitched using the written alphabet to make a desirable gift for a friend or relative.

The writing on the daisy picture is worked in back stitch using one strand of stranded cotton. Adapt the thread thickness to suit your chosen material. To check the thread, work a small section and then stand back to see if it is legible. If not, double the thread.

*Stitch count:* 138 × 115
*Design size:* 10 × 8in (25.5 × 20cm) Design as stitched, not as charted

MATERIALS *(See charts, pp42-3)*
*Unbleached linen: 30 threads to 1in (13 threads to 1cm)*
*Stranded cotton: 1 strand 936 (DMC) for the writing. See colour chart for clock face for colour key for the daisies*

To work the picture as illustrated adapt the chart as you stitch. The poem on the chart has been charted very tightly to enable it to fit on a page.

The worked example can be reproduced as follows.

Cut a piece of unbleached linen at least 17 × 15in (43 × 38cm), fold in four and press lightly. Sew a narrow hem around the material to prevent it from fraying and work two lines of tacking threads along the folds to find the centre. Where the two lines cross, stitch the word 'their' in one strand of dark olive green. Work the other words in the third line of the middle verse, allowing two complete squares between each word.

Now work the next line, up or down, allowing two squares between the extreme tips of the previous line. Work the rest of the poem, allowing seven clear squares between the verses.

When your poem is complete, the design may be decorated with suitable flowers or motifs. The daisies in the picture are taken from the clock face. Copy the designs from the clock face chart (p43), arrange in a pleasing position and stitch using the colours indicated.

When the project is complete, check for missed stitches and press on the wrong side. The design may then be stretched and framed as desired.

*Fig 18 Written alphabet*

*'To a Daisy', handkerchief case, napkin and daisy clock*

To a Daisy

There is a flower, a little flower,
With silver crest and golden eye,
That welcomes every changing hour,
And weathers every sky,

The prouder beauties of the field,
In gay but quick succession shine,
Race after race their honours yield,
They flourish and decline,

On waste and woodland, rock and plain,
Its humble buds unheeded rise,
The rose has but a summer reign,
The daisy never dies!

James Montgomery

# To a Daisy

There is a flower, a little flower,
  With silver crest and golden eye,
That welcomes every changing hour,
  And weathers every sky,

The prouder beauties of the field,
  In gay but quick succession shine,
Race after race their honours yield,
  They flourish and decline     plain,
On waste and woodland, rock and
  Its humble buds unheeded rise
The rose has but a summer reign,
  The daisy never dies!

James Montgomery

*To a Daisy*

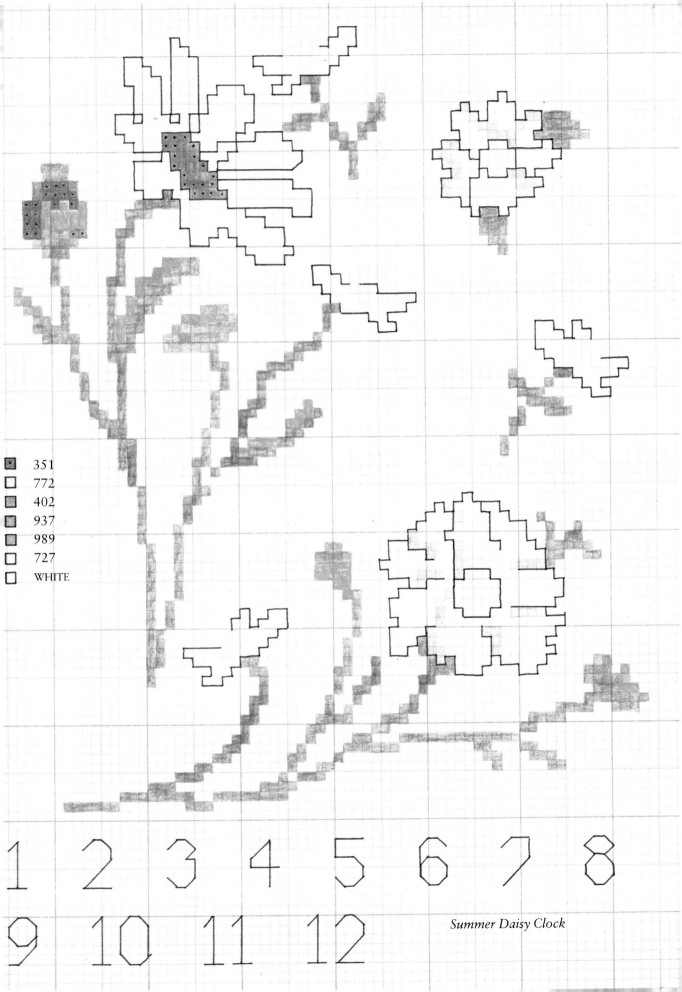

351
772
402
937
989
727
WHITE

1 2 3 4 5 6 7 8
9 10 11 12

*Summer Daisy Clock*

# HANDKERCHIEF CASE

This simple, but effective, case is a pretty solution to keeping hankies together in a drawer. The case is simply a folder, bound in ribbon and lined in a little luxurious satin.

*Stitch count:* 63 × 56
*Design size:* 5 × 4½in (12.5 × 11.5cm)

*MATERIALS (See chart opposite)*
*Linen in ivory: 25 threads to 1in (10 threads to 1cm)*
*Stranded cottons as on the chart*
*Medium-weight polyester wadding*
*Ivory or cream satin ribbon 2in (5cm) wide*
*Cream satin-backed crêpe for the lining*
*Narrow contrasting ribbon for the tie and bow*

Cut a piece of ivory linen 18 × 10in (45.5 × 25.5cm) and sew a narrow hem around all four sides. Fold the material in half widthways and lightly press. One of the sections will be the back and one the front. Now fold the front section in four and stitch a line of tacking threads along the folds to mark the stitching area.

Work the design from the chart, using two strands of stranded cotton for the cross stitch and one strand for the outlining and start in the middle.

When the needlework is complete, check for missed stitches and press on the wrong side.

Lay the completed design, face down, on a clean dry surface and cut a piece of polyester wadding a fraction larger than the linen. Using sewing cotton and large tacking stitches, sew the wadding to the wrong side of the worked piece.

Turn the design over so that the embroidered piece is facing you on the right side of the material. Cut a length of wide ribbon about 10in (25.5cm) long and lay this along the fold or 'hinge' of the case and pin in position. Fold the excess in to the inside of the case to be covered by the edge ribbon when complete. Stitch the edges of the ribbon through all the layers with tiny back stitches, catching the excess edges to the wadding on the inside.

Cut a piece of lining material slightly larger than the project and tack this to the inside on top of the wadding.

Cut a piece of wide ribbon which is long enough to go all the way around the linen material with a little extra for the turnings. To be sure of the dimension, measure your completed piece. Starting on a back section, pin the ribbon in place so that half the ribbon is visible on both sides. You should be able to stitch through all the layers and hem the two sides at the same time.

When the ribbon is stitched in place, fold the case in half and tie the narrow contrasting ribbon in position. Press with an iron to give it a finishing touch if required, but be careful not to flatten the polyester wadding.

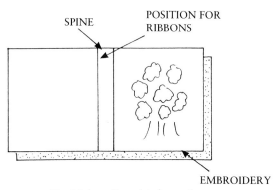

*Fig 19 handkerchief case layout*

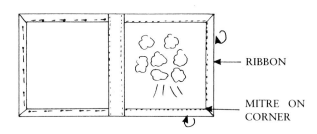

*Fig 20 Attaching the ribbon and lining
to the handkerchief case*

44

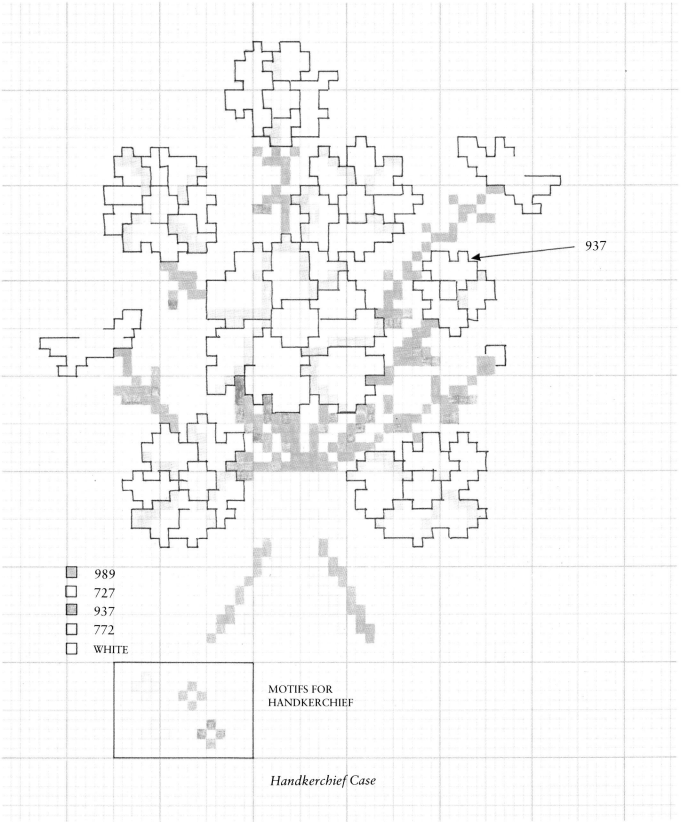

937

| | 989 |
| | 727 |
| | 937 |
| | 772 |
| | WHITE |

MOTIFS FOR
HANDKERCHIEF

*Handkerchief Case*

## HANDKERCHIEFS

The small hankies are made using the same technique as for the napkin. Choose a soft fine cotton. Add a triangle of linen or suitable even-weave material and work a small motif or two on the corners. They could be intended to complement the case or be on a different theme altogether. The small designs are included on the chart above.

# TABLE-NAPKIN

The body of the napkin is of a soft cotton which could not be used for counted cross stitch as it is not an even-weave material, so a section of Aida fabric is inserted in one corner.

*Stitch count: 40 × 35*
*Design size: 2¼ × 2in (5.7 × 5cm)*

*MATERIALS (See chart, p43)*
*Washable cotton material for napkin*
*A piece of matching Aida fabric 18 blocks to 1in (8 blocks to 1cm)*
*Stranded cottons as listed on the clock chart*
*Optional matching cotton lace 1in (2.5cm) wide*

Cut a piece of cotton material at least 18in (46cm) square, fold in a narrow hem along two sides and pin carefully. Using matching cotton thread, hem invisibly. Lay the hemmed piece on a clean dry surface with the two raw edges towards you. Pick up the unhemmed corner and fold this towards the middle. This is the section which will be cut off to be replaced by the Aida material. To check the size of the piece to be removed, measure the dimension from Point A to point B (see Fig 21), which should be 4¼in (11.5cm). Using sharp scissors, cut along the fold to remove the triangle of material. This shape may now be used as a pattern for the Aida. Lay the triangle of cotton fabric on the Aida and check that the even-weave

material is straight. Pin in position and cut out using sharp scissors.

Take the triangle of Aida and place on a clean flat surface with the point towards from you. Fold over a small hem on the two short sides and hem invisibly. Pin the lace around the hemmed edge and mitre the corner. Stitch invisibly in place. Join the triangle to the cotton fabric, matching the edges and trimming the seam allowance if necessary. Hem the remainder of the napkin edges to match the even-weave triangle. Once the napkin is complete, press lightly on the wrong side and proceed to the cross stitch.

The cross stitch daisy in the picture was adapted from the clock chart to fit the space available. Using one strand of stranded cotton or flower thread, work the design from the chart. Remember that table linen will need occasionally to be washed in hot water, so the thread must be colour fast.

HEM STITCHING

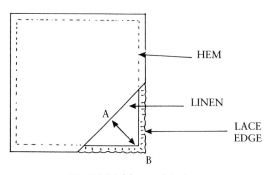

HEM

LINEN

LACE EDGE

A

B

*Fig 21 Table-napkin layout*

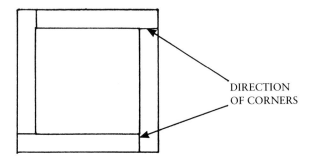

DIRECTION OF CORNERS

*Fig 22 Hem stitching and corner layout*

# CHAPTER 6

# Valentines and Sweethearts

This chapter includes cross stitch on paper, and decorated pin-cushions that do not need any embroidery at all. The Victorians loved a frothy, colourful look to their cards and gifts, as in the large heart-shaped pin-cushion (discovered in pristine condition in a local antique shop) in the top right of the picture overleaf. Such sweetheart cushions were often made by sailors when they were at sea. They would decorate small cushions with pins, beads, shells and sometimes pictures or other mementoes to remind their loved ones to wait for them. The heart-shaped cushion in the picture has ribbon, gold braid and cut-outs from greeting cards, all pinned in position. The two gorgeous modern pin-cushions illustrated in the picture (top right) were adapted from antique examples and are intended to inspire you to make your own beautiful versions.

## SWEETHEART PIN-CUSHIONS

Try adding sequins, ribbons, fabric flowers or even a special photograph to your own individual design. A sweetheart cushion could be adapted as a wedding or christening gift by using pastel colours, pearls and ribbon roses.

Use a firm medium-weight material for the cover of the cushion because it will need to keep its shape when it is fully stuffed. Cut a piece of material at least 1in (2.5cm) larger than the finished dimension to allow for the turnings. Place the right sides together, pin in position and sew around three sides of the cushion either with small back stitches or on a sewing-machine. Oversew or zig-zag the edges to prevent fraying and turn the pin-cushion right side out. Make sure that the corners are pushed out properly and press gently with a damp cloth. Stuff the cushion very firmly with polyester toy filling and slip stitch the open edge with strong matching thread.

To make sure that the pattern will look good on the cushion, but to avoid marking the material with too many alterations, first plan your design. Draw the initials or pattern on squared paper and then trace on to tissue paper. Remember, the design is drawn life-size. Stick the pins through the tissue paper and then remove the paper to reveal your masterpiece.

The examples illustrated use beads with a slightly iridescent sheen, but pearls or crystal beads or just sequins may suit your purpose. If you want to be really adventurous, try using oddments of lace cut out very carefully from old lace curtains or place-mats. They will only need to be pinned in place to be effective.

Using the pins, fix the beads to the cushion through the tissue paper until you can see the design developing. Pull away the paper and add the extra pins where necessary. Once you are satisfied with the beaded design, add any braid or fringing around the seams, again using pins and beads. If the cushion is for a bridal or christening gift, the edging could be made of layers of lace and ribbon.

*(previous page) Valentine fan novelty, card and sweetheart pin-cushions*

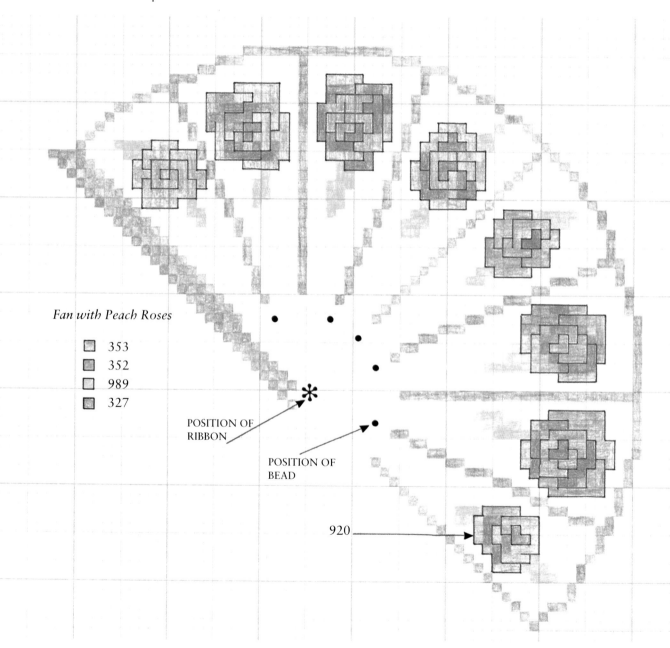

*Fan with Peach Roses*

- 353
- 352
- 989
- 327

POSITION OF RIBBON

POSITION OF BEAD

920

# FAN WITH PEACH ROSES

This novelty gift is stitched on white perforated paper, then cut out and decorated with beads and ribbon. For a Valentine, stitch the roses in a mixture of reds and greens. Gold or silver threads could be added for a Christmas greeting.

*Stitch count:* 61 × 64
*Design size:* 5 × 3in (13 × 7cm)

*MATERIALS (See chart opposite)*
*White perforated paper: 14 holes to 1in (6 holes to 1cm)*
*Stranded cottons as listed on chart*
*Narrow cream and peach ribbon*
*5 small leaf sequins*
*5 small embroidery beads*

Cut a piece of perforated paper at least 6in (15cm) square and stitch the design from the colour chart, referring to the guidelines on perforated paper on p21 if this is your first project on paper. Use three strands of stranded cotton for the cross stitch and two strands for the outlining. Work with clean dry hands as this sort of needlework cannot be washed (a soft rubber can sometimes save the situation).

When the design is complete, check for missed stitches and ensure that all loose ends are tied off. Using a sharp pair of scissors, carefully cut out the design following the cutting lines on the chart. Try to cut in one step each time and avoid sawing at the paper.

Lay the pastel-coloured leaf or similar type of sequin in a pleasing pattern over the ends of the solid lines on the pattern. These are held in place by stitching through a bead on the right side (see chart).

Cut two lengths of narrow ribbon, fold in half and stitch the centre to the point marked on the chart. Tie the ribbons in a pleasing bow and your gift is ready to give to someone special.

# VALENTINE CARD

*Stitch count:* 60 × 51
*Design size:* 4½ × 3¾in (11 × 9cm)

*MATERIALS (See chart overleaf)*
*Gold perforated paper: 14 holes to 1in (6 holes to 1cm)*
*Stranded cottons as listed on the chart*
*A paper doily*
*Ribbon (optional)*

Cut a piece of perforated paper at least 7in (18cm) square which will enable you to stitch the design and the writing on the same piece. Alternatively, the two sections may be worked separately.

Work the design from the chart, beginning in the centre and working outwards. The small amount of back stitch is added after the cross stitch is complete to define the hands a little more. When the cross stitch is complete, check for missed stitches and tie off any loose ends.

Cut out close to the stitching and fix to the doily using double-sided sticky tape. A ribbon may be attached to the back to hang the design or added at the bottom for decoration.

This pretty piece of Victoriana would look lovely stitched on black Aida and made up as a pin-cushion or special book-cover.

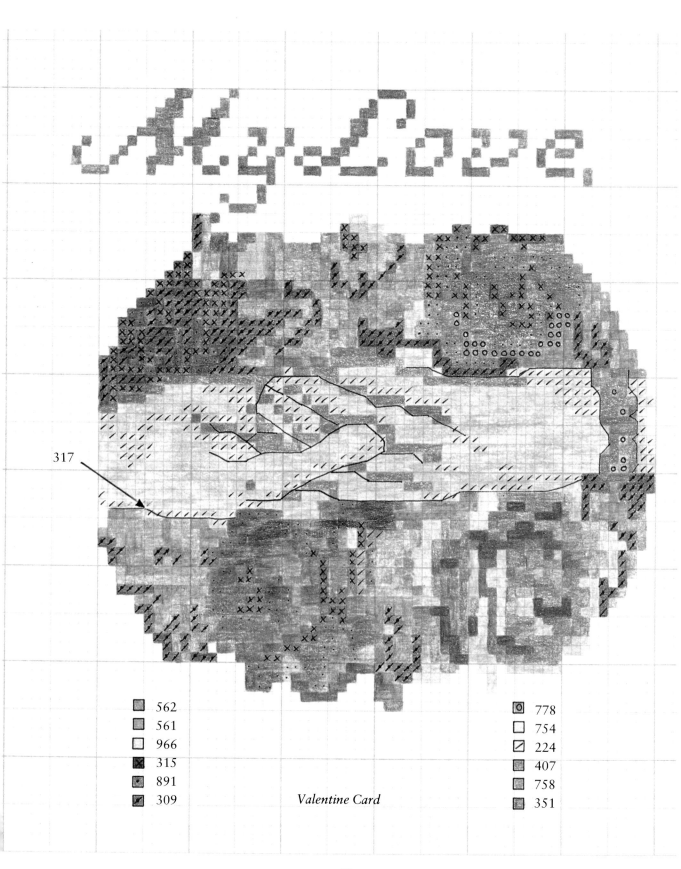

| | | | | |
|---|---|---|---|---|
| ▦ | 562 | | ◉ | 778 |
| ▢ | 561 | | ☐ | 754 |
| ☐ | 966 | | ▨ | 224 |
| ▧ | 315 | | ▦ | 407 |
| ▦ | 891 | | ▦ | 758 |
| ▧ | 309 | | ▦ | 351 |

317

*Valentine Card*

# VICTORIAN TIDY

This tidy is rather like an envelope with the seams left open. The folded material is held together with a matching ribbon tie in the centre, and the single flower was taken from the door-plate chart on p26. It makes a perfect gift-wrapping. A pair of lace handkerchiefs or some scented toiletries could be slipped inside as a lovely surprise.

The small flower motif is cut very close to the stitching because it has been treated with needlework finisher. This product, now readily available through most good craft shops, is a fabric stiffener, rather like a concentrated roller-blind conditioner. It can be applied to the front and back of the stitching without any ill effects.

*Stitch count:* 25 × 29
*Design size:* 1½ × 2in (3.5 × 5cm)

*MATERIALS (See chart, p26)*
*Linen in ivory: 30 threads to 1in (13 threads to 1cm)*
*Stranded cottons as listed on the chart*
*Matching satin ribbon ⅕in (5mm) wide for the edge*
*Narrow matching ribbon ⅒in (2.5mm) wide for the tie*
*Iron-on Vilene (interfacing)*
*Needlework finisher*

Cut a piece of linen at least 15in (38cm) square and over-sew the edge to prevent fraying.

Stitch one of the flowers from the door-plate chart using two strands of stranded cotton for the cross stitch. The position of the motif is very important as it will affect the shape of the 'tidy'. The design is centred horizontally, with the bottom corner 2½in (6.5cm) from the edge of the fabric (see Fig 23). When the stitching is complete, check for missed stitches and press lightly on the wrong side.

Cut a paper pattern 8in (20cm) square and place on top of the linen with the corner in the centre of the stitched motif. Note the arrows illustrating the direction of the grain of the linen. Draw around the pattern with tailor's chalk and remove the pattern. Cut a piece of iron-on Vilene (interfacing) large enough to cover the drawn pat-

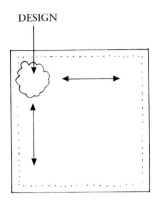

DESIGN

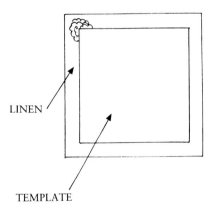

LINEN

TEMPLATE

*Fig 23 Position of the motif and template on tidy*

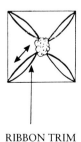

RIBBON TRIM

*Fig 24 Making up the tidy*

### Victorian Tidy

tern and the stitched motif. Fix the Vilene with a hot iron, checking that the linen does not wrinkle.

Using a little needlework finisher and a small toothbrush, paint the *front* of the embroidery and leave it to dry. This will seal the stitches and help to prevent them from fraying. Using sharp scissors, carefully cut out the square of linen following the line of tailor's chalk and cutting through all the layers as close as possible to the stitching.

Place the linen face up on a clean dry surface and cut a piece of ribbon 35in (89cm) long and pin to the edge of the linen, starting at one side of the cross stitch flower. Stitch the ribbon in position, either with small back stitches or using a sewing-machine.

Lay the fabric face down with the corner with the flower motif away from you. Thread a 'sharp' needle with matching thread and, lifting the corner opposite to the flower and the two side corners carefully, catch them together with a tiny stitch. Do not crease the material but keep the folds as soft as possible.

Cut a length of narrow ribbon, fold in half and invisibly stitch the centre point to the underside of the flower motif. Fold down the top or lid of the 'tidy', pull one of the lengths of ribbon through either side of the open section of the 'envelope' and tie in a neat bow.

# CHAPTER 7

# Christmas in Cross Stitch

The Victorians were the originators of many popular Christmas traditions, including the sending of cards and the decoration of the Christmas tree. We can re-create the spirit of those less commercial Christmases with personally made and stitched gifts, cards, gift-tags, covered boxes full of sweets and biscuits, and even an embroidered flower press.

This chapter gives a selection of Christmas ideas to inspire you to make your own gifts. The designs are planned to create a co-ordinated look. The cross stitch has been worked on linen, perforated paper and Aida to suit all tastes and can be mixed and matched for gift-tags, cards and table linen.

# PAPER TREE DECORATIONS

All these designs have been stitched on perforated paper and then cut out with sharp scissors. There are two ways of stitching designs that are intended to hang, either working two symmetrical pieces and sticking them together or working the design once and sticking coloured paper on the wrong side. The same principle would apply if you wished to make a Christmas mobile instead of tree designs.

## CHRISTMAS PRESENTS
*Stitch count:* 20 × 24
*Design size:* 1½ × 1¾in (3.5 × 4.5cm)

*MATERIALS (See chart, p58)*
*White perforated paper*
*Stranded cottons as listed on the chart*
*Gold thread to hang design (optional)*

Refer to the general guidelines and instructions on p21 before you start to make your presents.

Cut a piece of perforated paper at least 2½in (6.5cm) square and, using the chart on p58, work the Christmas present using three strands of stranded cotton for the cross stitch and two strands for the outlining. These designs have been worked in traditional Christmas colours, but you can easily improvise and incorporate your own colour scheme.

When the embroidery is complete, carefully cut out the present along the cutting lines shown on the chart. Cover the back of the stitching with a second stitched 'present', using double-sided sticky tape. If you intend to use the design as a gift-tag for a special present, cover the back with some plain paper using a small amount of rubber-based adhesive. As you will see from the picture, two small gift-tags have been stitched by adapting a section of the Christmas present chart. These 'bow' designs were stitched on off-cuts of paper, and the names were worked using the basic alphabet on p40.

## CHRISTMAS PUDDING AND CRACKER
These are worked in exactly the same way as the presents, although the cracker is worked on gold perforated paper. Some of the design on the cracker is left unstitched so that the glitter of the paper will show through.

## BEADED GARLANDS
*Stitch count:* 26 × 27
*Design size:* 2 × 2in (5 × 5cm)

*MATERIALS (See chart, p58)*
*White perforated paper*
*Stranded cottons as listed on the chart*
*Small gold beads*

Cut a piece of perforated paper at least 3in (7.5cm) square and, using the chart on p58, stitch the design using three strands of stranded cotton for the cross stitch and two strands for the outlining. Work all the cross stitch and outline before adding the gold-coloured beads as shown on the chart. Add the beads using a fine 'sharp' or beading needle and a half cross stitch and one strand of matching thread. If your beads are not the same size as the examples used in the picture, use as many as you like. Although the two garlands illustrated are worked in different colour-ways, the actual shape of the motif is still symmetrical and therefore may be stuck together, back to back.

The design for this simple garland has been used for a card, this time without the beads, and using red stranded cotton for the berries. Instructions for making a card are included at the end of the chapter.

*Tree decorations*

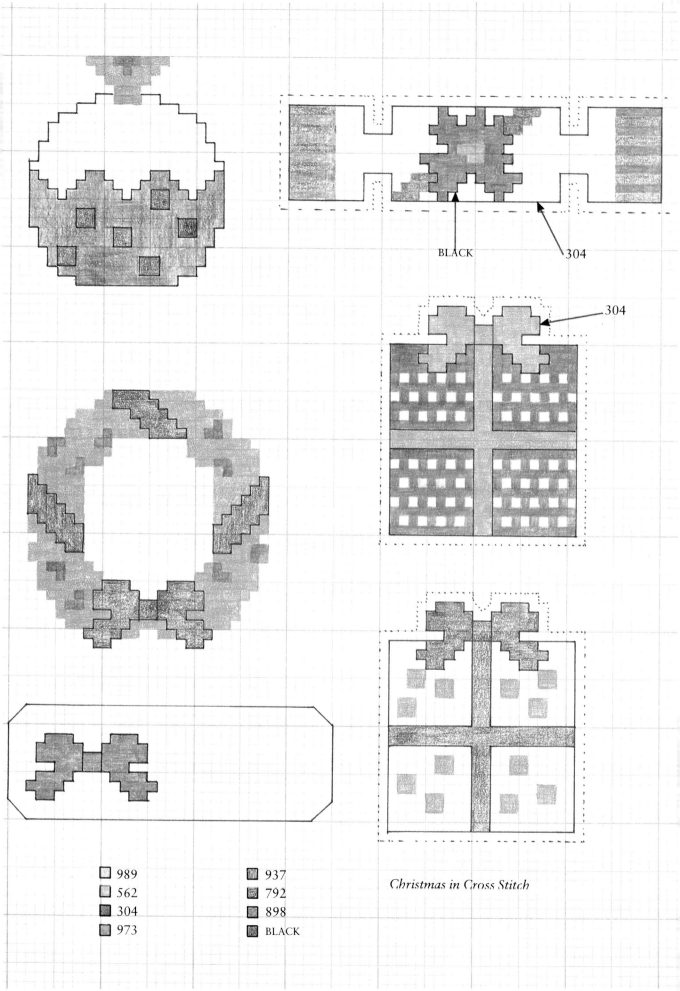

BLACK

304

304

| | 989 | | 937 |
| | 562 | | 792 |
| | 304 | | 898 |
| | 973 | | BLACK |

*Christmas in Cross Stitch*

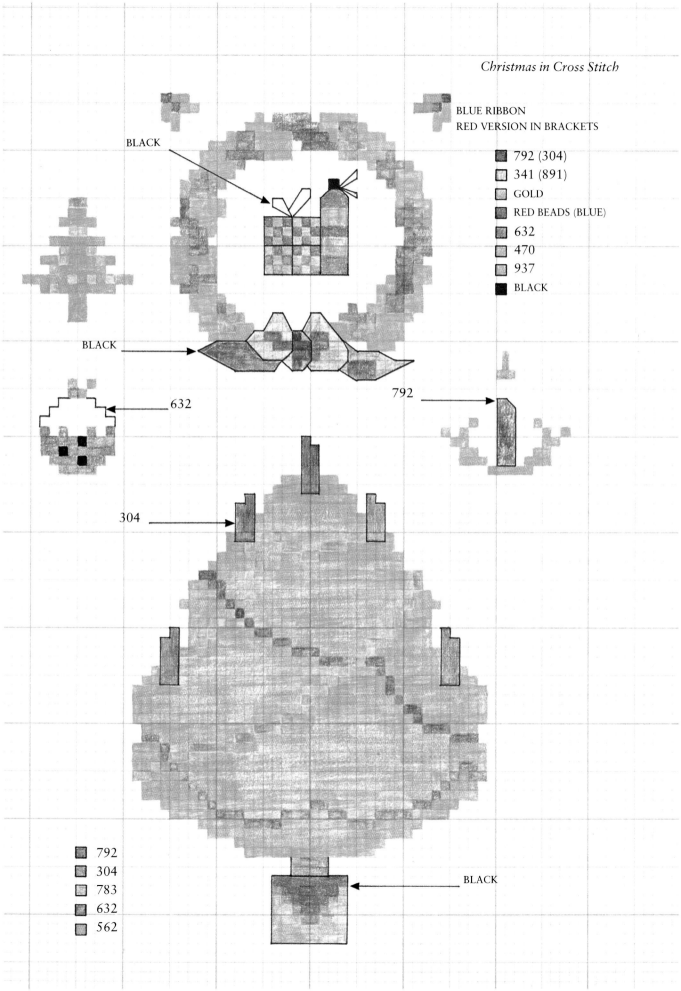

*Christmas in Cross Stitch*

BLUE RIBBON
RED VERSION IN BRACKETS

BLACK

792 (304)
341 (891)
GOLD
RED BEADS (BLUE)
632
470
937
BLACK

BLACK

632

792

304

BLACK

792
304
783
632
562

# CHRISTMAS
# TABLE SETTING

For a really special Christmas table setting, the 'present' design has been adapted for a set of napkins and napkin-rings. These designs are simple to do, but look effective when stitched in bold primary colours. If you would like a more sophisticated feel to your table settings, adapt a single flower or Christmas rose, adding a metallic thread or blending filament for extra sparkle.

The cross stitch on the napkins has been worked in German Flower Thread, using one strand for both the cross stitch and the outlining. The place-name is worked on the same idea as the gift-tags in the previous section except that the paper was cut large enough to allow the label to be folded so that it will stand on its own.

## TABLE-NAPKINS

*Stitch count:* 20 × 24
*Design size:* 1½ × 1¾in (3.5 × 4.5cm)

*MATERIALS (See chart, p58)*
*Linen in ivory: 30 stitches to 1in (13 stitches to 1cm)*
*German Flower Threads as listed on the chart*
*Strong matching linen thread*

Decide how large you would like your napkins to be. The examples illustrated are 18in (46cm) square, allowing a little for the narrow hem. When cutting the linen, check that the material is straight by pulling a thread and trimming the fabric to match.

Fold a narrow hem allowance cleanly and in a straight line. By far the most successful way of doing this is to 'score' the material. Place the linen on a clean flat surface with the wrong side facing you. Count the threads for your hem allowance and place a needle in between the threads, where you wish the fold to occur. Holding the needle firmly in your right hand, pull the material (not the needle) steadily with your left hand, scoring the material as you go. You will find that the hem will fold into position easily and in a straight line. Stitch the hem. Hem stitching is used to decorate

the right side, making a pretty row of holes evenly spaced along the hem, as well as finishing off the raw edge. Always use a thread of the same weight as the fabric; if necessary, you can pull threads from the linen edge. The example illustrated demonstrates hem stitch counting two threads of the material. As long as the same count is used along the length of the hem, this could be increased to three or even four threads if wished. See Fig 22 (p46) for hem stitching around corners.

When the napkins are hemmed, press lightly on the wrong side and stitch the design of your choice in one corner. The cross stitch on the linen napkins was worked in German Flower Thread. To position the motif, count diagonally from the corner of the hemmed napkin and stitch from the corner of the chart and work inwards.

When the cross stitch is complete, check for missed stitches and outline as necessary using a contrasting thread. Press lightly on the wrong side and the napkin is ready for use.

## NAPKIN-RINGS

*Stitch count:* 20 × 24
*Design size:* 1½ × 1¾in (3.5 × 4.5cm)

*MATERIALS (See chart, p58)*
*Perforated paper in white*
*Stranded cottons or Flower Thread as chart*
*Double-sided sticky tape*

The Christmas present chart has been adapted yet again for these excellent napkin-rings. The design may be stitched in the same colour-way as the table linen, or mixed and matched as you prefer.

Cut a piece of perforated paper at least 2½ × 6½in (6.5 × 16.5cm) and work the design in the centre. When the design is complete, work a line of back stitch along the two long sides, leaving one

*Table setting with napkins, napkin-rings, cracker and pop-up Christmas tree card*

60

complete row of unused holes between the design and the back stitch. Using a pair of sharp scissors, cut along the two long edges, using the row of holes next to the back stitch as a cutting line.

When the stitching is complete, the paper strip will need to be bent into a tube shape. The best way to do this is to wrap the stitched piece gently around a rolling-pin or something similar. This makes a smoother shape and keeps the paper from creasing in the wrong place. To fix the paper in position, overlap the two ends and, using double-sided sticky tape, press firmly together.

# CRACKER, CHRISTMAS CARD AND NOVELTIES

The pop-up Christmas tree card had some small sparkly stars added after the design was stitched. The bright blue cracker was made out of available material and the Christmas motif was worked on even-weave material, then stitched to the cracker fabric and filled with after-dinner mints.

## CHRISTMAS CRACKER
*Stitch count:* 32 × 32
*Design size:* 1¾in (4.5cm) square

*MATERIALS (See chart, p59)*
*Bright blue material (but not necessarily even weave) for the cracker*
*Aida fabric: 18 blocks to 1in (8 blocks to 1cm)*
*Stranded cottons as listed on the chart*
*Small blue glass beads*
*Silver lace ¾in (1.5cm) wide*
*Cardboard tube (an empty toilet roll is ideal)*
*Double-sided sticky tape*

Measure the length and circumference of the cardboard tube and add 6 in (15cm) to the length and 1in (2.5cm) to the circumference. Using these dimensions, cut out a piece of brightly coloured material for the cracker.

Cut a piece of Aida material at least 3in (7.5cm) square and oversew the edges to prevent fraying. Work the little garland design from the chart, adding the small glass beads with a 'sharp' or beading needle, using a half cross stitch for each bead. The garland is illustrated in different colourways with other central designs on the card and the book pocket. Making up instructions for these two projects are included at the end of the chapter.

When the stitching is complete, check for missed stitches and press lightly on the wrong side. Fold under a narrow hem and tack in place on the centre of the cracker material. Using small back stitches and matching thread, stitch the little square of material to the cracker fabric. Lay the design face up on a clean dry surface, and fold under a narrow hem on the two short sides of the cracker material (see Fig 25). Pin the narrow lace along the hem-line and, using small back stitches, sew through all the layers.

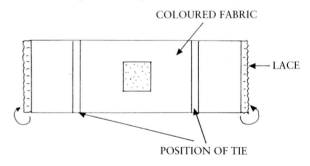

COLOURED FABRIC

LACE

POSITION OF TIE

*Fig 25 Making up the cracker*

Take the cardboard tube and rule a line along its length with a soft pencil marking the centre. Stick a piece of double-sided tape along the pencil line and peel off the backing. Mark the centre of the long side on the cracker material and match this to the mark on the cardboard tube, carefully

*Three-fold Christmas cards and book pocket*

sticking the material in position. If you intend to put sweets in the cracker (wrapped peppermint creams are ideal) push them inside the tube, and carefully roll the tube inside the material, folding in the last raw edge and sticking with double-sided tape. Using matching threads or ribbon, tie either side of the tube into a cracker shape and hide until it is needed.

## POP-UP CHRISTMAS TREE CARD
*Stitch count:* 53 × 38
*Design size:* 2½ × 3¾in (7 × 9.5cm)

*MATERIALS (See chart, p59)*
*Silver and gold perforated paper*
*Stranded cottons as listed on the chart*
*Star-shaped sequins*
*Stiff card or black perforated paper for the stand*
*Double-sided sticky tape*

Cut a piece of silver perforated paper at least 5in (13cm) square and stitch the tree design from the chart on p59. The whole tree is stitched using three strands of stranded cotton for the cross stitch and adding the little star sequins on top of the cross stitch.

When the tree is stitched, cut it out following the guidelines on the chart and set aside. Stitch an assortment of little Christmas presents using oddments of paper and threads. Cut these out and set aside.

Cut a strip of black paper or stiff card ¾in (1.5cm) wide and 6in (15cm) long. Mark the centre and place the base of the tree over the mark. Stick in position with double-sided tape, adding the presents on either side. Make sure that the card does not show from the front by trimming as necessary and set aside while you make a stand.

Cut a piece of stiff card as wide as your stitched group and fold exactly in half. Open out the card, lay a length of double-sided tape along the inside of the fold and stick the two sections together. Open out the card again as far as possible and fold

the remaining flaps back on themselves, thus making the fixed section stand on its own. Using sticky tape, fix the mounted stitched group to the stand and adjust the card until the design stands unaided.

## BOOK POCKET
Measure the book intended for the pocket and add at least 2in (5cm) to all the dimensions. Cut two pieces of brightly coloured material (or one on the fold) for the pocket. (The material does not have to be even weave.) With the right sides together, stitch round using either small back stitches or with a sewing-machine. Oversew any raw edges, turn to the right side and press lightly. The same design as the cracker was stitched on a piece of Aida and that in turn was stitched to the front of the pocket. The edges were covered with a matching ribbon trim and the book was slipped inside. If you wish, a ribbon handle could be added and the pocket hung on the Christmas tree.

## THREE-FOLD CARDS
Purchased card 'blanks' are available from most craft and needlework shops and are ideal for cross stitchers. A design may be stitched on material of your choice and inserted into many types of card. The most common variety is the 'three-fold' kind which includes a flap to stick down when the design is in position. The design is fixed in place using either rubber-based adhesive or double-sided tape, making sure that the design is in the centre of the opening on the front.

The small garland designs included in this chapter are excellent motifs for inclusion in cards as they may be personalised by adding an initial or name in the centre.

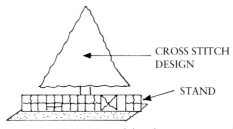

CROSS STITCH DESIGN

STAND

*Fig 26 Stand for the pop-up card*

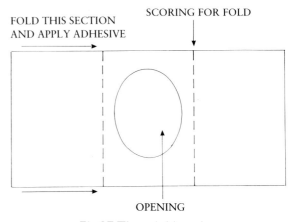

FOLD THIS SECTION AND APPLY ADHESIVE

SCORING FOR FOLD

OPENING

*Fig 27 Three-fold cards*

# CHAPTER 8

# *Lace and Pot-pourri*

The combination of lace and pot-pourri is almost always successful – add a little cross stitch on linen and you have a perfect gift. Always choose lace or embroidered net that blends well with your even-weave material. If possible, use cotton lace and look for ivory or 'old white' shades rather than white. Most nylon lace is brilliant white and tends to make linen look grubby.

## ROSE-SCENTED SACHET

This frothy rose-scented sachet has cross stitch over one corner of the linen with some surface lace and two lace frills. For best value, make two sachets, as the lace triangle is just a square divided in half.

*Stitch count: 55 × 55*
*Design size: 5 × 5in (13 × 13cm)*

MATERIALS (See chart, p68)
*Linen in ivory: 25 threads to 1in (10 threads to 1cm)*
*Triangle of surface lace in ivory*
*30in (76cm) of 1in (2.5cm) lace flounce*
*30in (76cm) of 2in (5cm) lace flounce*
*7in (18cm) of ³⁄₄in (2cm) lace flounce*
*Stranded cottons as listed on the chart*
*Pot pourri for filling*

Cut a piece of linen at least 7in (18cm) square and sew a narrow hem around the edges to prevent fraying. Cut another piece for the back and set aside (a piece of suitable backing material could be used for the back). Take the linen square and fold in four *diagonally* and press lightly. Sew a line

of tacking threads along these folds to help position the lace and the cross stitch.

Stitch the little rosebuds from the chart, working the design from the middle, but from corner to corner. When the cross stitch is complete, add the back stitched trellis lines in between the rosebuds. Check for missed stitches and press lightly on the wrong side.

Lay the completed cross stitch on a clean dry surface with the right side up. Position the cross stitch in the top right-hand corner. Cut a piece of lace at least 7in (18cm) square, cut in half diagonally and set one piece aside. Lay one triangle of lace over the unstitched section on the linen and pin in place (shown on the chart as point A and point B). Fold the short length of lace flounce in half lengthways and lay it along the lace triangle, sliding the raw edges of the lace inside the fold. Pin in position carefully and stitch through all the layers using small back stitches. Fold under a small seam allowance all the way around the linen square and press lightly with a warm iron. Join and gather the narrow lace flounce and finish off any raw edges. Pin this to the wrong side of the

65

linen square, tack in position keeping the gathers as even as possible. Do the same for the wide flounce and pin this behind the first frill and tack in place.

Using the spare piece of linen or backing material, fold under a narrow seam allowance to match the stitched square. Lay this on the top of the cross stitch, with the wrong sides together, matching the sides and the corners.

Using matching thread and small back stitch, sew through all the layers, leaving a small gap for the filling. (This could be done on a sewing-machine.) Add your choice of pot-pourri and finish off the seam securely. A ribbon may be added if the sachet is intended to hang in a cup-board.

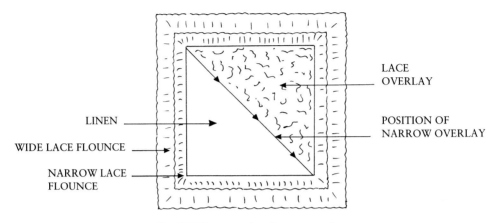

*Fig 28 Diagram for the rose sachet*

# SCENTED SLEEP PILLOW

This pillow is filled with rose petals, powdered cloves and variegated minted leaves – a wonderful aid to relaxation. You could make your own combination of favourite scented petals and stitch a matching flower on the linen.

*Stitch count:* 50 × 74
*Design size:* 8 × 11½in (20 × 29cm) – completed pillow size

*MATERIALS (See chart, p69)*
*Linen in ivory: 25 threads to 1in (10 threads to 1cm)*
*Surface lace in ivory*
*39in (1m) of 1in (2.5cm) lace flounce*
*78in (2m) of 2in (5cm) lace flounce*
*9in (23cm) of ¾in (2cm) lace flounce*

*45in (114cm) narrow ribbon in dusky pink and sage green*
*Stranded cottons as listed on the chart*
*Pot-pourri for filling (see below)*
*Muslin bag*

Cut two pieces of linen at least 13 × 10in (33 × 25cm) and sew a narrow hem around the edges to prevent fraying. Set one piece aside for the back and fold the remaining section in two and press lightly. Stitch a line of tacking threads along the fold to help position the stitching and the lace.

Lay the linen on a clean flat surface with the long side towards you. The cross stitch design is worked in the right-hand section of the linen (see

*Rose-scented Sachet and Sleep Pillow*

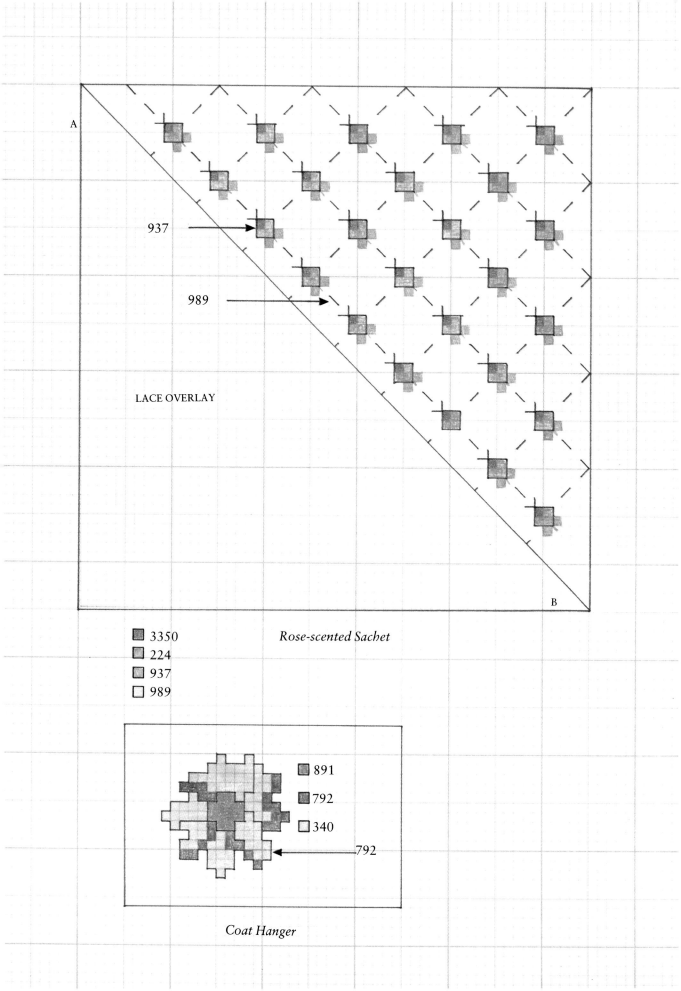

A

937

989

LACE OVERLAY

B

■ 3350
■ 224
■ 937
□ 989

*Rose-scented Sachet*

■ 891
■ 792
□ 340

792

*Coat Hanger*

3350

937

| | |
|---|---|
| ☐ | 988 |
| ☐ | 937 |
| ☐ | 223 |
| ☒ | 3350 |
| ☐ | 225 |
| ☑ | 818 |
| ☑ | 224 |
| ☐ | 948 |

*Scented Sleep Pillow*

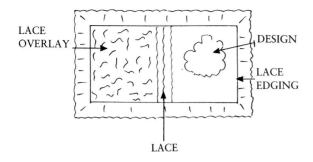

*Fig 29 Sleep pillow layout*

Fig 29). Following the chart, stitch the rose design using two strands of stranded cotton for the cross stitch.

When the cross stitch is complete, check for missed stitches and press lightly on the wrong side.

Lay the embroidery on a clean flat surface with the right side of the stitching facing you. Cut a piece of surface lace large enough to cover the unstitched half of the linen and pin in position. Lay the short piece of lace along the raw edge of the lace and pin carefully. Using matching thread and small back stitches, sew through all the layers. Fold under a narrow seam allowance and press

lightly. Join the ends of the wide lace flounce, finish any raw edges, gather and pin to the edge of the embroidered linen and tack in position. Use the narrow flounce to cover the gathered edge, pinning and tacking in position. Take the piece cut for the back and fold in and press a narrow seam allowance to match the embroidered section. Pin in position, matching the corners. Using matching thread and small back stitches, sew through all the layers, leaving a small gap for the herbs.

As it is possible that this project may need to be washed eventually, it is worthwhile using a muslin bag for the herbs, which can then be removed when the outer cover is washed.

To make the pot-pourri for the sleep pillow, you will need about 1pt (570ml) dried rose petals, 1oz (25g) bruised cloves and two large spoonfuls of dried mint (not the sort bought in spice jars – pick some mint leaves and hang them to dry naturally). Mix the leaves together well and put inside a muslin bag. Pop this inside your stitched cover and sew up the gap.

Once complete, add the little ribbon bows at each corner and give the pillow to someone special.

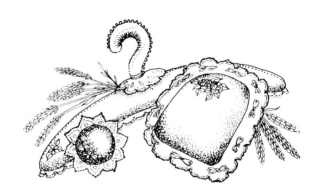

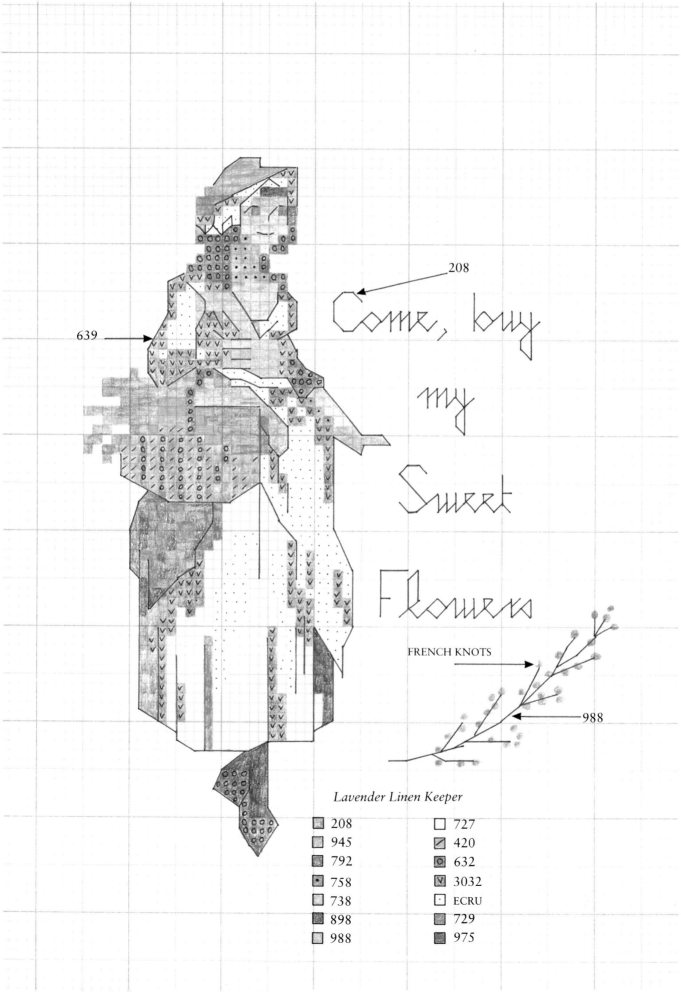

208

639

Come, buy my Sweet Flowers

FRENCH KNOTS

988

Lavender Linen Keeper

| | | |
|---|---|---|
| 208 | | 727 |
| 945 | | 420 |
| 792 | | 632 |
| 758 | | 3032 |
| 738 | | ECRU |
| 898 | | 729 |
| 988 | | 975 |

# LAVENDER LINEN KEEPER

This design for a simple lavender bag may well seem familiar because the flower seller is used as a trade mark by the well-known Yardley cosmetics company. If you are giving this as a gift, maybe you could fill the bag with lavender soaps or bath salts.

*Stitch count:* 73 × 58
*Design size:* 5 × 4in (12.5 × 10cm)

*MATERIALS (See chart opposite)*
*Linen in sage green: 30 threads to 1in (13 threads to 1cm)*
*Stranded cottons as listed on the chart*
*13in (33cm) of cotton lace ³⁄4in (2cm) wide*
*20in (50cm) lilac satin ribbon*
*Dried lavender or lavender pot-pourri for filling (see below)*

Cut two pieces of linen at least 7 × 10in (18 × 25cm) and set one piece aside and oversew the raw edge of the other. Working from the chart, stitch the cross stitch design using two strands of stranded cotton for the cross stitch and one strand for the outlining. Complete the cross stitch before you add the back stitch outline which sits on top of the cross stitches in some places. Add the writing in one strand of stranded cotton and add the lavender flowers using French knots (see Fig 48). When the stitching is complete, check for missed stitches and press on the wrong side.

With the right sides together, pin and tack three sides of the bag. Sew the two pieces, either using a sewing-machine or sew by hand in small back stitches. Turn the bag the right way out and press with a damp cloth or steam iron. Fold in a narrow hem along the top of the bag and tack in position. Join the ends of the lace, gather and pin to the inside edge of the bag. Stitch through all the layers using matching thread and small back stitches.

Fold the ribbon in half and, using a small stitch, catch it to one of the side seams. Fill the bag with lavender and firmly tie the top. If you want to make your own pot-pourri for this project, you will need a cupful of each of the following: freshly stripped lavender flowers, dried thyme and mint leaves. Just mix them all together and add a tablespoonful of coarse salt, powdered cloves and caraway seeds. Keep in an air-tight tin until the pot-pourri is needed.

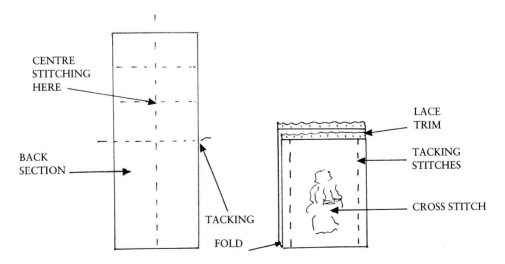

*Fig 30 Making up the lavender linen keeper*

# PERFUMED COAT-HANGER

This project is a great favourite as it is so simple to make yet so effective. The little flower motif is actually adapted from the daisy flowers on the handkerchief case on p45. The daisy is charted in blue but you could stitch it in any colour-way. The secret is to co-ordinate the ribbons for the hook with the threads used for the cross stitch. The flower is worked seven times, evenly spaced along the hanger, but each alternate flower is worked upside down so that it appears to be a different shape.

The polyester wadding is perfumed by placing it in a polythene bag full of lavender for a few days, but you could add the scent of your choice. A variety of perfumed oils are readily available from chemists and beauty shops, but do check that the oil will not stain your material.

*Stitch count:* 13 × 13
*Design size:* depends on the coat-hanger

*MATERIALS (See chart, p68)*
*Non-metal coat-hanger*
*Linen in ivory: 30 threads to 1in (13 threads to 1cm)*
*Stranded cottons as listed on the chart*
*3/4in (2cm) lace flounce (length depends on the hanger)*
*20in (50cm) narrow satin ribbon in two shades*
*Extra ribbon in one of the shades to cover the hook*
*Medium-weight polyester wadding (perfumed as above)*

First make a pattern of the hanger. Place the hanger in the middle of a sheet of paper and draw around it with a pencil. Remove the hanger and add 1½in (4cm) all the way around. Cut out the pattern carefully and fold it in half to mark the centre. Place the pattern on a piece of linen and pin in position. Make sure that the threads in the linen are vertical and horizontal before you cut out two hanger shapes. Work the first flower in the centre of the linen shape and then evenly space each re-

*Perfumed Coat-hanger*

maining flower, if necessary measuring to check the position as you go. Work each flower using two strands of stranded cotton for the cross stitch and one strand for the back stitch outline. When the embroidery is complete, check for missed stitches and press on the wrong side.

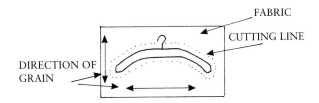

*Fig 31 Cutting the material for the coat-hanger*

Using the paper pattern, cut two pieces of polyester wadding and place these on either side of the body of the hanger, pinning and tacking in place. You may find that it is easier to do this if you remove the hook until it is needed.

To estimate the amount of lace needed, measure the distance from the hold for the hook all the way around the hanger and back to the hook, adding a 2in (5cm) margin.

Fold in a narrow seam allowance on the embroidered piece of linen and do the same with the back section. Starting slightly to the left of the centre top, pin the lace to the wrong side of the embroidery, easing the lace around the corners. Pin and tack in position.

Cover the hook by wrapping it in one of the satin ribbons, starting at the top and working down the hook, folding the ribbon around the base of the hanger before knotting firmly. Lay the embroidered section face down on a clean dry surface and place the hanger on top, making sure that it is in the centre. Add the back section, folded side innermost, and pin one to the other every inch (2.5cm) or so. Check that the body of the hanger is enclosed by the material. Using matching thread and small back stitches, sew through all the layers, working from the front and leaving a small gap around the hook. Fold the remaining ribbons in half and tie them around the base of the hook.

# CHAPTER 9

# *Victorian Lilies*

This versatile lily was adapted from a Berlin wool chair-seat pattern. The design has also been used for the Beaded Lily Purse in Chapter 10 and could be adapted to fit a picture frame. The four pretty lilies on the crystal pot are actually the same simple lily design worked at different angles around a central point with a little greenery in back stitch. The brooch and the card are the same design again, but a single flower has been stitched on black fabric.

# LILY TRAY

The soft subtle colours chosen for the lily tray make it ideal for a dressing table, or even a drinks tray. The shape of the finished piece will depend upon the choice of tray. The purchased tray is also ideal for holding your needlework. Before you cut the material for the lily, check the thread count and stitch count and make sure that the stitched piece will fit easily under the glass.

*Stitch count:* 115 × 77
*Design size:* 7 × 4¾in (18 × 12cm)

*MATERIALS (See chart, p78)*
*Linen: 34 threads to 1in (14 threads to 1cm)*
*Stranded cottons as listed on the chart*
*Purchased tray*

If you are planning to use a purchased tray, take it apart carefully and read the manufacturer's instructions. Unless otherwise indicated, the best way to proceed is to use the base of the tray as a pattern to cut the fabric to the right size allowing at least 2in (5cm) all the way around. Work the design from the chart using two strands of stranded cotton for the cross stitch and one strand for the back stitch outline.

When the embroidery is complete, check for missed stitches and press lightly on the wrong side. Following the manufacturer's instructions, make up the tray as illustrated.

*Lily Tray*

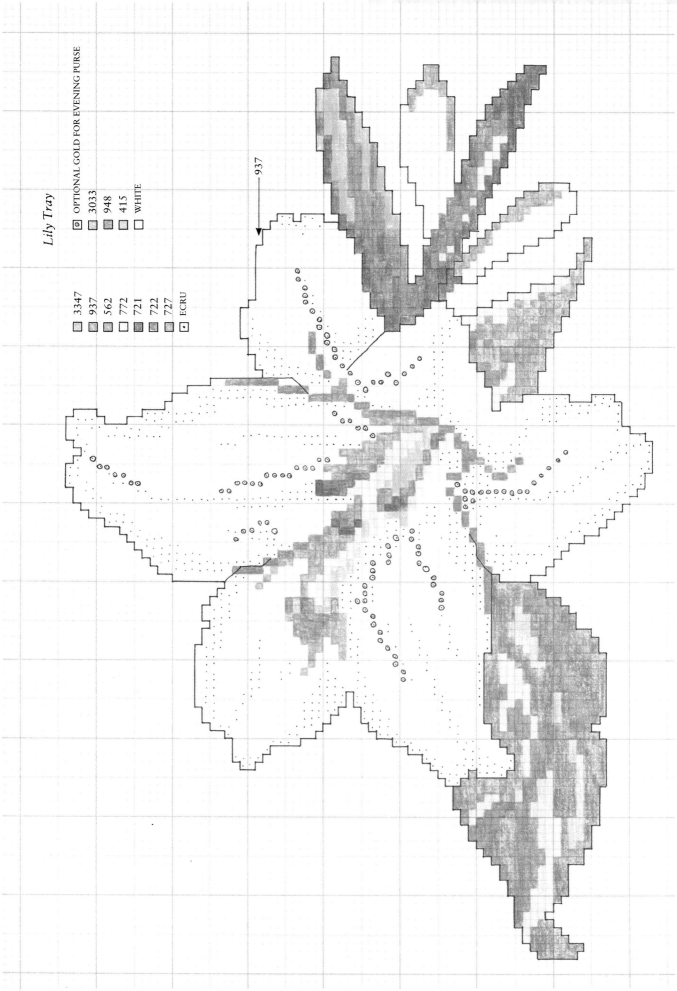

*Lily Tray*

OPTIONAL GOLD FOR EVENING PURSE
3033
948
415
WHITE

3347
937
562
772
721
722
727
ECRU

937

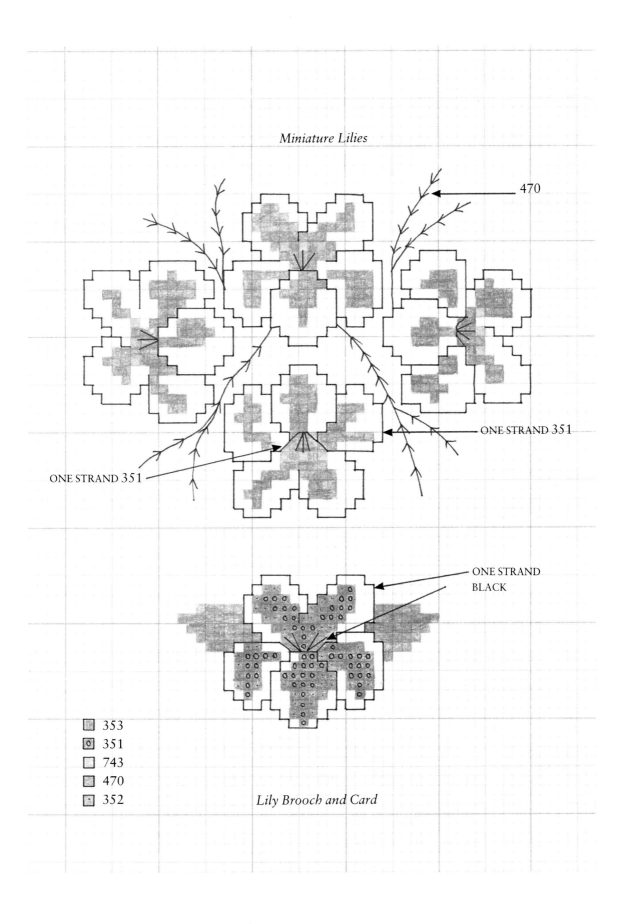

*Miniature Lilies*

470

ONE STRAND 351

ONE STRAND 351

ONE STRAND
BLACK

353
351
743
470
352

*Lily Brooch and Card*

# MINIATURE LILIES

The crystal trinket pot has provided a lovely setting for the four little lily heads set among a little back stitched greenery.

*Stitch count:* 48 × 34
*Design size:* 2 × 1½in (5.5 × 3.75cm)

*MATERIALS (See chart, p79)*
*White Hardanger: 25 blocks to 1in (10 blocks to 1cm)*
*Stranded cottons as listed on the chart*
*Purchased crystal pot*

Choose a suitable crystal or porcelain trinket pot and, using the lid as a guide to the size, carefully cut a piece of material for the design, adding at least 1in (2.5cm) all the way around. Work the design from the chart using one strand of stranded cotton for both the cross stitch and the back stitch. When the embroidery is complete, check for missed stitches and press lightly on the wrong side. Make up the trinket pot following the manufacturer's instructions.

# LILY BROOCH AND CARD

These two projects are worked by adapting one of the lilies from the crystal pot and adding two simple leaves. Both designs are stitched on the same black even-weave material. The difference in size in the two projects is achieved by working the cross stitch over two threads in the card and only one thread in the purchased brooch.

*Stitch count:* 28 × 16
*Design size:* depends on the method used for the project

*MATERIALS (See chart, p79)*
*Black even-weave fabric: 28 threads to 1in (12 threads to 1cm)*
*Stranded cottons as listed on the chart*
*Purchased brooch or card*

Cut a piece of material large enough for your choice of project allowing at least 1in (2.5cm) all the way round. Work the single lily from the chart.

If you are making the card, work the cross stitch over two threads in each direction using two strands on stranded cotton, adding the outline in one strand of black in back stitch.

If you are making a small brooch, work the cross stitch over one thread in each direction using just one strand of stranded cotton for both the cross stitch and the outline. To do this you will need to complete each cross stitch as you go rather than in two journeys.

When the cross stitch is complete, the design can be made up into a brooch following the manufacturer's instructions. The instructions for making up a three-fold card are given on p64.

*Miniature Lilies on a crystal pot, with the Lily Card, Brooch, and (overleaf) Golden and Arum Lilies*

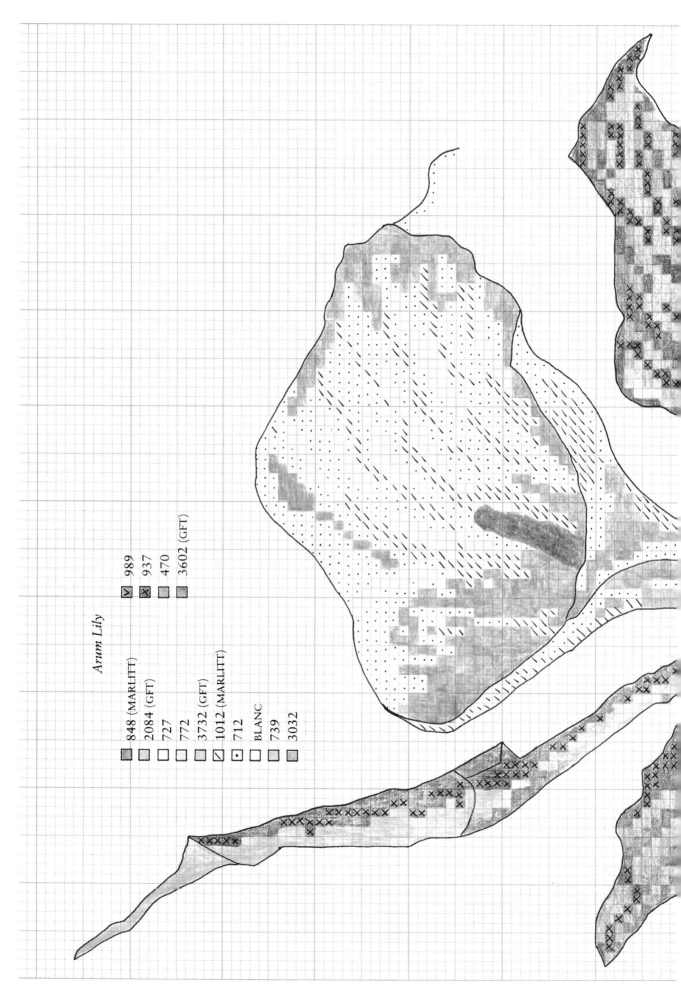

*Arum Lily*

| | |
|---|---|
| ■ | 848 (MARLITT) |
| ■ | 2084 (GFT) |
| □ | 727 |
| □ | 772 |
| ■ | 3732 (GFT) |
| ▨ | 1012 (MARLITT) |
| · | 712 |
| □ | BLANC |
| □ | 739 |
| ■ | 3032 |

| | |
|---|---|
| ☒ | 989 |
| ☒ | 937 |
| ■ | 470 |
| ■ | 3602 (GFT) |

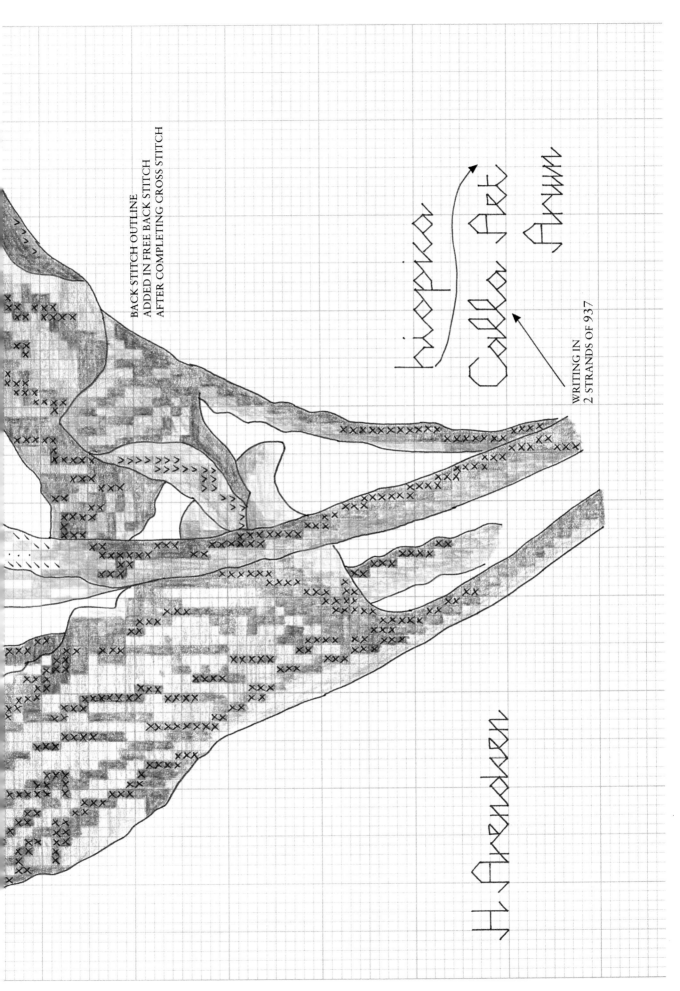

BACK STITCH OUTLINE
ADDED IN FREE BACK STITCH
AFTER COMPLETING CROSS STITCH

WRITING IN
2 STRANDS OF 937

Ethiopica
Calla Art
Arum

H. Arendzen

SINGLE STRAND 937

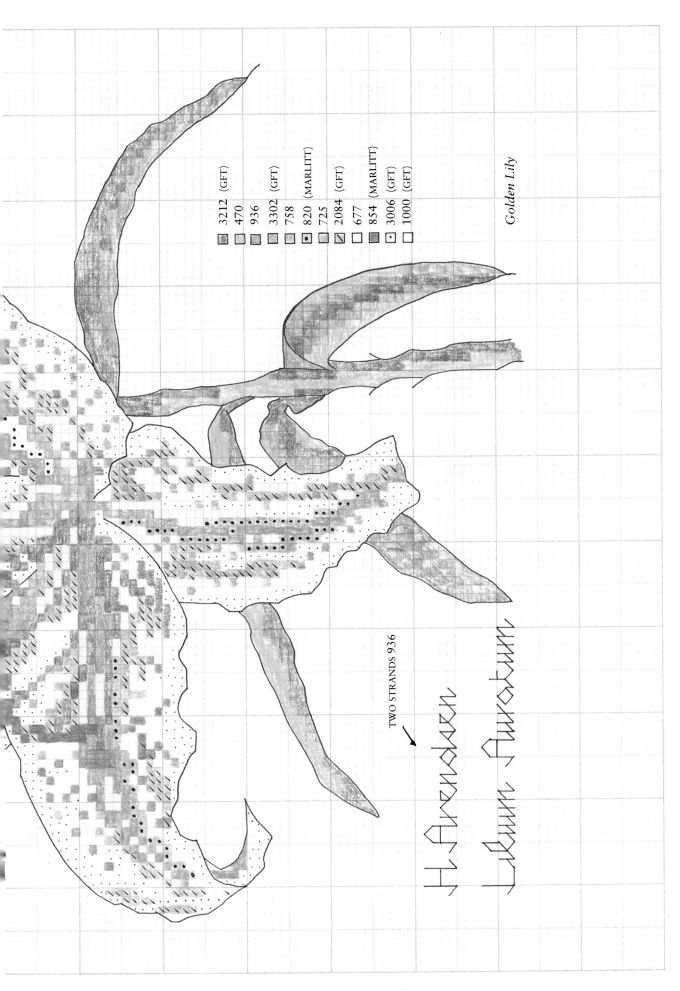

3212  (GFT)
470
936
3302  (GFT)
758
820  (MARLITT)
725
2084  (GFT)
677
854  (MARLITT)
3006  (GFT)
1000  (GFT)

*Golden Lily*

TWO STRANDS 936

H. Arendsen
Lilium Auratum

# GOLDEN AND ARUM LILIES

These beautiful lilies have been carefully copied from exquisite hand-coloured illustrations found in a book at the Natural History Museum in London.

## LILIUM AURATUM
*Stitch count:* 130 × 105
*Design size:* 8½ × 7in (21.5 × 18cm)

## CALLA AETHIOPICA ARUM
*Stitch count:* 131 × 102
*Design size:* 8½ × 7in (21.5 × 18cm)

The materials and instructions below relate to both designs, intended as a pair.

*MATERIALS (See charts, pp84-7)*
*Unbleached or natural linen: 30 threads to 1in*
  *(13 threads to 1cm)*
*Stranded cottons (number only on chart)*

*Marlitt rayon thread (Marlitt on chart)*
*German Flower Thread (GFT on chart)*

Cut a piece of linen at least 18 × 16in (46 × 41cm) and sew a narrow hem to prevent fraying. Fold the linen in four and press lightly. Stitch a line of tacking threads along the folds to mark the centre of the material.

Work the lily, starting in the centre using the different yarns as indicated on the chart. For the cross stitch, use two strands of stranded cotton, two strands of Marlitt and one strand of Flower Thread, adding the back stitch outline in one strand of Flower Thread or stranded cotton. When the cross stitch is complete, add the name of the artist in two strands of stranded cotton as shown on the chart. Once complete, press the embroidery on the wrong side and stretch and mount (see p21).

# CHAPTER 10

# Bouquets and Beads

The design on the splendid evening bag (overleaf) comes from a Berlin chart, adapted to match a pink silk ball-gown. A small matching purse or cosmetic case is worked using part of the design. You could also work a single flower on the corner of a lace handkerchief (see p45).

The ivory-coloured top and fastening for the bag, found in an antique market, was attached to a filthy old brocade bag. The bag was dismantled and the top was scrubbed in non-biological detergent before it was used. If you have no luck in finding an old example, modern varieties are available, or you could effectively adapt a pair of bell-pull handles.

The choice of a cream linen background makes the bag suitable for many different occasions, but the design could be stitched on a black fabric or even worked in wools with your own choice of background colour.

The Beaded Lily Purse is an example of counted cross stitch worked on a black material. This is the simplest design to do: it is worked in cross stitch except for a few beads to add a little glitz. The chart is actually the design for the Lily Tray with some adaptions and the fabric is Aida.

The Wreath of Roses pin-cushion is a good example of how effective a simple cross stitch pattern can look when it is stitched in black linen. The secret when working on fine black linen is to do as much as possible in daylight unless you have a light fitting with a daylight bulb.

The Rose Pendant is stitched on cream Aida with the background covered in cross stitch. This is unusual with counted cross stitch but is still very effective. The design was worked and then the black was added to fit the silver locket. Again, this is an example where the design could be stitched in alternative colours to match a particular dress or blouse.

# ROSES EVENING BAG

*Stitch count:* 130 × 100
*Design size:* 8²/₃ × 6²/₃in (22 × 17cm)

MATERIALS (See chart, p92-3)
*Cream linen: 30 threads to the inch (13 threads to 1cm) (see below for the allowance for the back and gusset)*
*Stranded cottons as listed on the chart*
*Matching lining fabric (cream curtain-lining was used in the model shown)*
*Heavy-weight sew-in Vilene (interfacing)*
*Matching cotton thread (for making up)*
*Bag top*

First cut the fabric to the right size. You will need the piece for the design plus turnings, the same for the back and a little for the gusset.

If you are using a 30 thread linen as in the model illustrated, the dimensions will be as below. Allow more if you are using a fabric with a lower thread count.

*Front and back:* 9 × 11in (23 × 28cm)
*Gusset:* 17 × 3in (43 × 7.5cm)

Sew a narrow hem around the material to prevent fraying, fold into four and press lightly. Work a line of tacking threads along the fold lines, following the threads in the fabric. Work the design beginning at the centre of the chart as shown. When complete, check for missed stitches and press the embroidery on the wrong side.

Making up will depend on the type of top and bag fastening that you have obtained, although the basic principles will be the same. First, make a paper pattern from your stitched piece by laying the needlework on a clean sheet of paper and carefully pinning the design to the paper. Turn over and draw a line with a soft pencil around the design, following the shape of the stitching, adding ³/₄in (1.5cm) for turnings (make sure that the eventual size of the bag will fit *your* bag top). Remember, you will be stitching close to the embroidery so you do not need a large margin. Using the paper pattern, trim the embroidered

piece to match and cut out a fresh piece for the back. Cut a strip of linen for the gusset (dimensions given above).

Trim about ¹/₂in (1.5cm) all the way around the paper pattern and cut a piece of Vilene (interfacing) to match each of the linen shapes. The interfacing helps to give the linen body and also prevents the turnings from showing through the bag. Lay a piece of interfacing on each linen shape

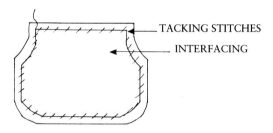

*Fig 32 Stitching the interfacing to the material*

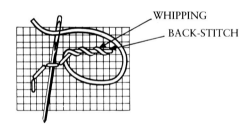

*Fig 33 Whipping back stitch*

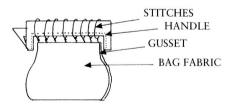

*Fig 34 Holding the handle in position*

*Roses Evening Bag*

937
562
470
472
3687
602
309
894
600
224

3685
966 +BLANC
966

*Roses Evening Bag*

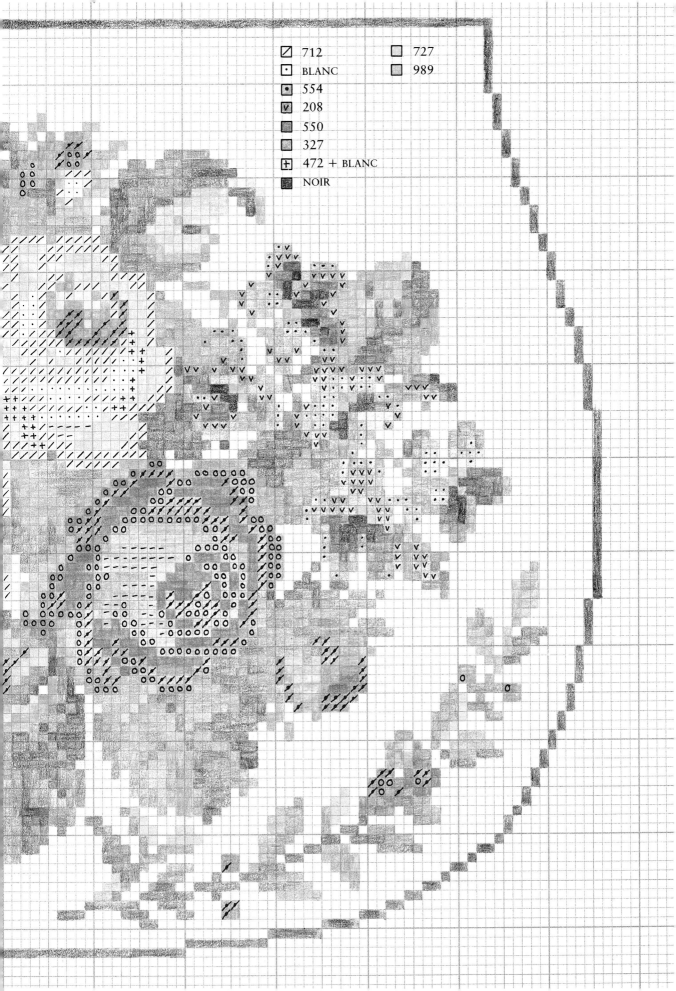

712
BLANC
554
208
550
327
472 + BLANC
NOIR

727
989

on the wrong side, fold the turning allowance over the interfacing and tack in place. Catch the turnings to the interfacing using straight stitches at right angles to the raw edge.

The three pieces are joined together rather like a patchwork, working from the wrong side, using matching strong cotton thread and stitching as close as possible to the black outline on the front.

The purpose-made bag tops have small holes punched along the underneath of the fitting, to which the needlework is stitched using small back stitches. In the example illustrated, cream silk was used for the back stitch which was then whipped with more of the same to give the impression of a cord framing the edge. When making up, the black line at the top of the design did not suit the shape of the old fastening, so it was decided to cover it by the fitting. When back stitching, it is helpful to hold the work in position with temporary long stitches over the handle and then these are removed before the lining is added.

The lining was stitched over interfacing and made up as before, except that you could make a small mirror pocket in the lining fabric before it is slipped inside the bag and ladder stitched along the top using a curved needle. The top edge of the lining can be covered with a suitable braid which can be stitched invisibly when the bag is complete. The bag may need a handle or cord depending on the sort of fitting you have acquired. It can be most attractive to make the cord from colours already in the design.

To make a twisted cord, decide how long you want the finished cord to be (for a shoulder- or hand-bag), then double this measurement for the length of yarn required. The idea is to hold both ends fairly taut and to keep twisting. This job is easier if another person holds the other end. Eventually, if you walk towards each other, the cord will twist together on its own.

# WREATH OF ROSES PIN-CUSHION

*Stitch count:* 50 × 50
*Design size:* 3½in (9cm) in diameter

*MATERIALS (See chart, p98)*
*Linen in black: 26 threads to 1in (11 threads to 1cm)*
*Stranded cottons as listed on the chart*
*Hard-wood pin-cushion base and pad*
*Matching strong cotton thread*

Cut a piece of linen 7in (17.5cm) square. Tack a narrow hem around the fabric, fold into four and press lightly. Tack in fold lines in light-coloured thread and stitch the design following the chart. Work from the centre as usual, counting to the nearest rose and then following the pattern around. Remember, you can turn the work around 180° and work the design with the top stitch still facing the same way. Never turn just 90° because the stitch will be formed incorrectly.

If you plan to give this pin-cushion as a gift, it would be simple to stitch an initial from the Victorian alphabet on pp34-5 in the centre of the wreath or garland. If the letter you require has a violet rather than a rose illustrated, draw your own as follows. Using graph paper (10 squares to 1in (2.5cm) is ideal), draw the letter without a flower. Separately, copy the rose you like from the chart on pp34-5. Now, carefully cut out the rose and place it on top of the letter until you like the position. Draw around the cut shape and colour in with crayons. To stitch the letter, centre the design as usual and, using colours from the wreath, add to the pin-cushion design.

Once the wreath is complete, check for missed stitches and press lightly on the wrong side. Do not remove the tacking stitches yet as they will be useful when you complete the cushion.

The hard-wood pin-cushion base used for this design can be obtained from most good needle-

## Wreath of Roses Pin-cushion

work shops. The cushion pad is usually removed by undoing the screw underneath the wooden base and the stitching is then applied before reassembly.

Measure your cushion pad carefully and roughly mark the centre, then, using the tacking threads as a guide, push a pin through the centre of the stitched piece and match this with the pin in the pad. This will ensure that the design is in the centre. Using glass-headed pins, secure the needlework along the base of the pad and, once you are satisfied that there are no wrinkles or tucks in the fabric, stitch invisibly through the fabric and the pad. Remove all the pins and check for unnecessary folds and pleats. Only when you are com-

pletely satisfied should you trim away any excess fabric leaving enough to tuck underneath. Add the base, tuck the fabric inside and tighten the screw provided.

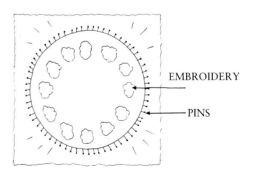

*Fig 35 Making up the pin-cushion*

# ROSE PENDANT

*Stitch count:* 30 × 30
*Design size:* 1¾in (4.5cm) in diameter

*MATERIALS (See chart, p98)*
*Aida fabric: 18 blocks to 1in (8 blocks to 1cm)*
*Stranded cottons as listed on the chart*
*Purchased silver pendant*

Cut a piece of Aida fabric 2½in (6.5cm) square and over-sew the raw edge to prevent fraying. Stitch the design from the chart using just one strand of stranded cotton for the cross stitch. When the flowers are complete, decide if you wish to add the black background. If so, add cross stitches in one strand of black over all vacant blocks of Aida. Check the design inside the pendant until you are satisfied with the result. When complete, check for missed stitches and press on the wrong side. Make up the pendant according to the manufacturer's instructions, checking that the design is straight inside the fitting before you seal it up.

# BEADED LILY PURSE

*Stitch count:* 92 × 77
*Design size:* 6½ × 5½in (16.5 × 14cm)
*Completed purse dimensions:* 14 × 8in
  (35.5 × 20cm)

*MATERIALS (See chart, p78)*
*Stranded cottons: as for the lily tray (page 78)*
  *unless you are using the beads*
*Small glass beads: Mill Hill beads were used for*
  *the model in the picture*
*Black Aida: 14 blocks to 1in (5 blocks to 1cm);*
  *(see below for fabric requirements)*
*Black satin or silk lining fabric*
*Medium-weight polyester wadding*
*Matching strong black cotton for making up*

Before cutting the black Aida, decide on your bag size and whether you intend to make a clutch bag or one that will hang on a cord.

To make the purse illustrated, cut a piece of Aida 16 × 26in (40.5 × 66cm) and fold the fabric into three, tack along fold lines and also straight down the middle of all three sections.

The stitching is worked in the bottom third of the fabric, starting on the tacking line in the centre of the fabric and working the lily off-centre. Work the design from the chart, leaving out the lower large leaf.

If you wish to use beads as in the illustration, simply replace the following stranded cottons with small glass beads. As long as the beads are approximately the same size as the cross stitches on the rest of the design, you should have no problems.

| DMC Stranded Cotton | Mill Hill Beads |
| --- | --- |
| 415 | Grey (150T) |
| 772 | Pale green (561T) |
| 948 | Gold or bronze (57T) |
| 727 | Yellow (128T) |
| 721 | Orange (423) |

You may find it easier to stitch some of the cross stitch before adding the beads using a 'sharp' sewing or beading needle and a half cross stitch. The secret is to make sure that all the beads face the

*Beaded Lily Purse and Rose Pendant*

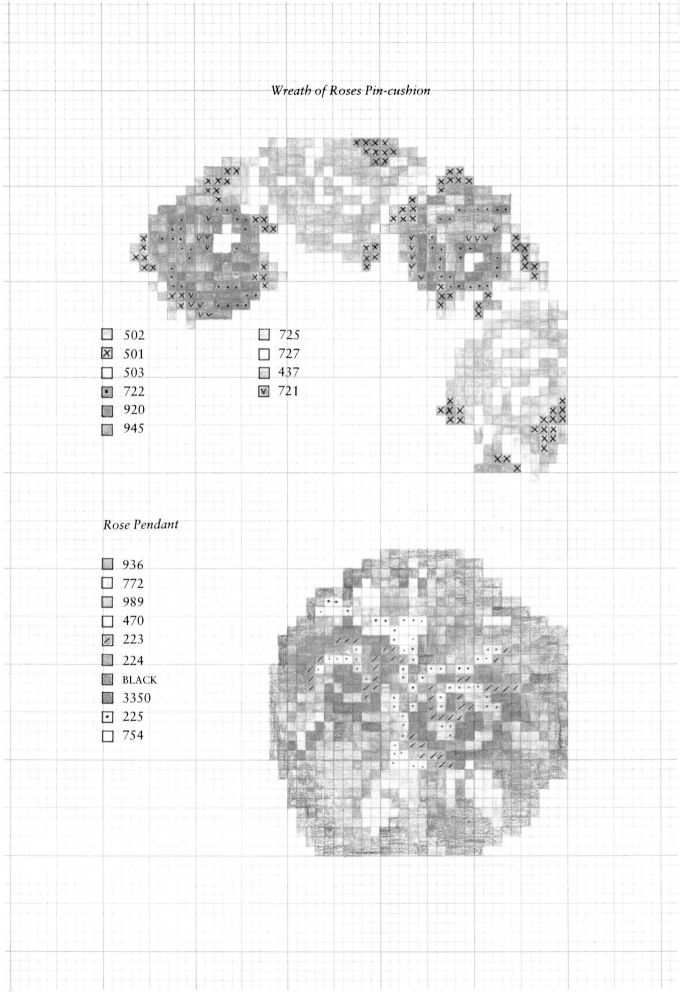

*Wreath of Roses Pin-cushion*

| | |
|---|---|
| ☐ 502 | ☐ 725 |
| ☒ 501 | ☐ 727 |
| ☐ 503 | ☐ 437 |
| ▪ 722 | ⱱ 721 |
| ▨ 920 | |
| ▨ 945 | |

*Rose Pendant*

☐ 936
☐ 772
☐ 989
☐ 470
▨ 223
☐ 224
▨ BLACK
▨ 3350
▪ 225
☐ 754

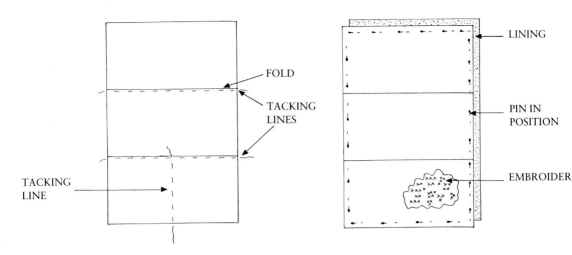

Fig 36 *Layout of tacking threads for evening purse*

FOLD

TACKING LINES

TACKING LINE

LINING

PIN IN POSITION

EMBROIDER

Fig 37 *Attaching the lining to embroidery*

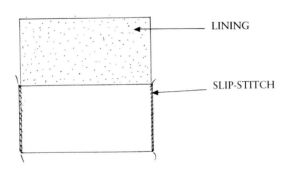

LINING

SLIP-STITCH

Fig 38 *Making up the evening purse*

same way and that you fasten off well every few stitches.

When the lily is complete, check for missed stitches and press on the wrong side with a warm iron. Avoid pressing too hard as the fabric will crinkle around the beads. Dampen it slightly or use a steam iron and then leave to dry before making up. Fold in ¾in (1.5cm) turning all the way round and tack in place.

Lay the needlework face down on a flat clean surface. Cut a piece of polyester wadding slightly smaller than the Aida and place on the wrong side of the stitching, tacking in place. Now cut a piece of the lining fabric 16 × 26in (40.5 × 66cm) and tack through all the layers.

Folding the raw edges inside as you go, slip stitch the lining to the black Aida, checking that there are no puckers or wrinkles on the right side. Remove all the tacking stitches and press lightly. Lay the lined purse on a clean flat surface with the embroidery at the top, face down. Fold the bottom edge upwards and pin in place.

Check that the embroidered section will fold down neatly, and, once you are satisfied with the effect, stitch the sides of the bag invisibly. The design illustrated does not include a fastener, but a press stud or a matching ribbon tie would be suitable. If you wish to add a cord, either make a twisted cord as described above or buy a suitable light-weight curtain cord.

# CHAPTER 11

# *Floral Bedchamber*

For anyone who ever dreamed of a romantic Victorian bedroom, here is a selection of projects to help create that dream. The patchwork quilt is put together by sewing-machine, but a cross stitch design is added to the centre of each section to make it a true original. The embroidered design on the nightdress case was adapted from a page in a Victorian photograph album and the dressing-table set uses small motifs from the quilt design.

# LILY NIGHTDRESS CASE

The cross stitch pattern used for the nightdress case is charted on p103, but you may wish to plan your own design to match bedding or wallpaper. As you will see later in this chapter, it is simple to adapt a pattern from a printed fabric and to make a cross stitch chart which will enable you to co-ordinate the colours and patterns in any room and to match any style of furnishing.

*Stitch count:* 102 × 58
*Design size:* 6½ × 3½in (16.5 × 9cm)

*MATERIALS (See chart, p103)*
*Linen in 'old' white: 30 threads to 1in (13 threads to 1cm)*
*Stranded cottons as listed on the chart*
*Marlitt rayon threads as listed on the chart*
*3in (7.5cm) wide lace flounce in old white*
*Polyester wadding in medium weight*
*Matching satin lining*
*29in (74cm) rose-pink satin ribbon ¼in (6mm) wide*
*20in (50cm) rose-pink satin ribbon ⅛in (3mm) wide*

When choosing materials for this project, try to buy the lace and the linen together if possible. The colour of white lace and linen varies considerably and the completed work will look much more effective if the two materials blend well.

Cut a piece of linen, satin lining and a piece of polyester wadding at least 24 × 15in (61 × 38cm). Take the lining and wadding and set aside until they are needed.

You will need to fold the linen in three sections to plan the correct position of the cross stitch design. Lay the linen on a clean flat surface with a narrow edge towards you. Fold the linen into three sections and work a line of tacking threads along the three folds. Now fold the material in half longways and sew a line of tacking threads along this fold, on one third section only, to enable you to position the design which is stitched off-centre. Two rows of four-sided stitch will then make a soft fold for the 'hinge' of the case (see p32). When you look at the chart you will see that the lace will compensate for the narrow linen

*Lily Nightdress Case*

100

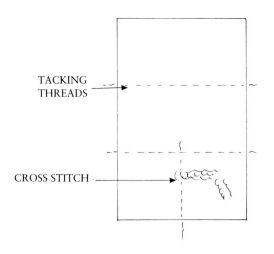

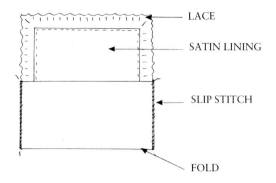

Fig 40 Attaching the lining to the
embroidery

Fig 39 Tacking threads for the
nightdress case

section. Once the design has been positioned correctly, you may begin stitching, working from the chart. The cross stitch is worked in two strands of stranded cotton and two strands of Marlitt. The small amount of outline is worked in one strand of stranded cotton in the shades shown on the chart.

When the cross stitch is complete, work two rows of four-sided stitch along the tacking line above the embroidery, using either strong linen thread or threads pulled from the linen itself. Check for missed stitches and press lightly on the wrong side.

Lay the embroidery face down on a clean dry surface and fold in a narrow seam allowance all the way round and tack in position. Lay the piece of wadding on top of the linen and trim to fit. Tack in position. Lay the lining material on top of the wadding, with the wrong sides together, and, folding the raw edges inside, pin all the way round enclosing the wadding completely. Slip stitch the linen to the lining fabric invisibly using matching thread and small stitches.

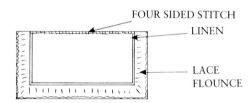

Fig 41 Making up the nightdress case

Lay the project on a clean flat surface with the embroidery face up, gather the lace flounce and carefully pin it to the bottom edge of the embroidered section of the nightdress case. Tack in place. Using the wider ribbon, place it on top of the lace edge and, with matching thread, carefully stitch the ribbon and lace in place.

To complete the nightdress case, fold up the bottom section to make the pocket and slip stitch up the sides using matching thread and small stitches. Press very lightly. Be careful not to press too hard as the polyester wadding will flatten very easily. Add two small ribbon bows for the corners and all you need is the nightdress to go inside.

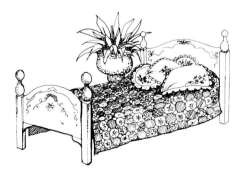

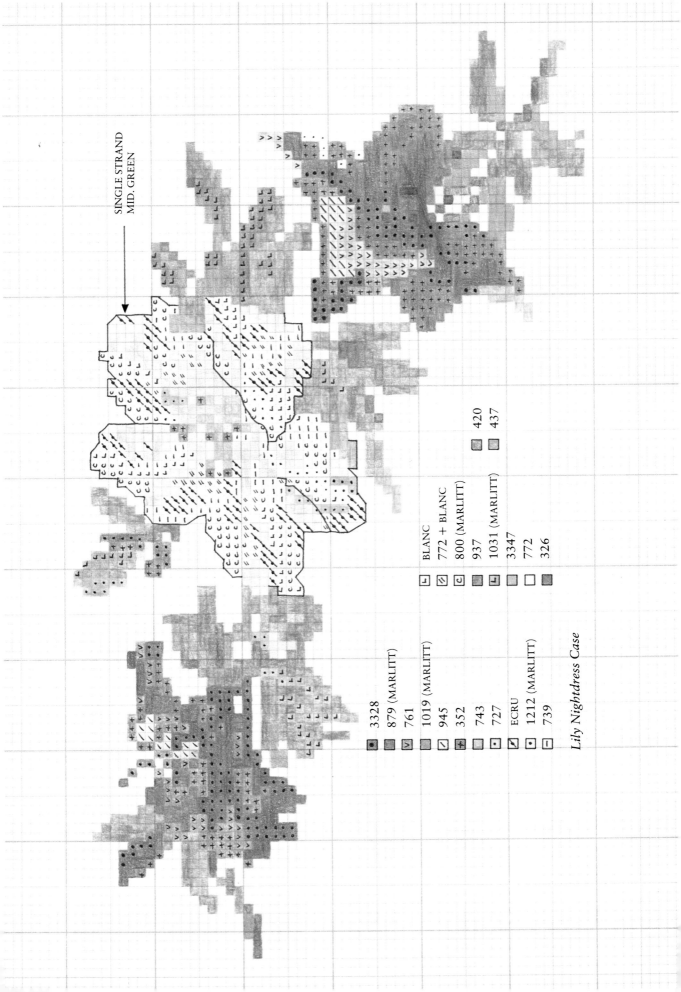

SINGLE STRAND
MID. GREEN

- ⌐ 3328
- ▨ 879 (MARLITT)
- ⩔ 761
- ▨ 1019 (MARLITT)
- ⟋ 945
- + 352
- ▨ 743
- ⊡ 727
- ⟋ ECRU
- ⊡ 1212 (MARLITT)
- − 739

- ⌐ BLANC
- ▨ 772 + BLANC
- ⊏ 800 (MARLITT)
- ▨ 937
- ⌐ 1031 (MARLITT)
- ▨ 3347
- ▢ 772
- ▨ 326

- ▨ 420
- ▨ 437

*Lily Nightdress Case*

# PATCHWORK QUILT

This log-cabin patchwork is made from two Liberty lawn prints. Each section has a cross-stitched motif based on the Liberty designs. (See the two photographs of the quilt, opposite and previous page.) The charts for the designs are included on p108, but you may wish to plan your own cross stitch pattern to go with your choice of material. If so, choose two fabrics, one with a dark and one with a light background. Trace off the design onto squared paper, then square it up and colour with crayons. Remember that the size of the finished motif will depend on the stitch count of your materials.

The quilt is made up of 16 squares, each of which measures about 21in (53cm). Each square is made up of one small square of embroidered linen measuring 2½in (6cm) and strips of cotton lawn joined together as shown in Fig 42.

*MATERIALS (See chart, p108)*
*Linen in ivory: 30 threads to 1in (13 threads to 1cm)*
*Stranded cottons as listed on the chart*
*Printed cotton material for the patchwork*
*Matching cotton for the sewing-machine*
*Cotton sheeting for the lining*

Cut 16 pieces of linen at least 4in (10cm) square and oversew the edges to prevent fraying. Following the charts, work the designs using two strands of stranded cotton for the cross stitch and one for the back stitch outline. A few French knots are added to the flowers and are worked in two strands of cotton.

When the embroidery is complete, check for missed stitches and press lightly on the wrong side.

Cut strips of the cotton material. Test first, but you may find that you can snip the edge of the fabric and tear the strips rather than cut them out. Cut or tear an equal number of strips 3in (7.5cm) wide from the printed fabrics and sort into different piles or boxes.

Following the patchwork layout, join the pieces together using a sewing-machine and allowing ½in (1cm) seam allowance, pressing the seams as you go. Eventually, you will have 16 squares which can be joined together to make one double-bed cover. The best way to proceed is to lay pieces out on the floor to plan the position and direction of each section before you pin and stitch them together. When the quilt is made up, line with cotton sheeting.

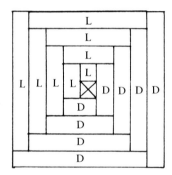

L = LIGHT BACKGROUND

D = DARK BACKGROUND

× = DESIGN POSITION

*Fig 42 Log cabin patchwork layout*

(previous page) Patchwork Quilt

(opposite) Dressing-table Set

106

# DRESSING-TABLE SET

These lovely pots were purchased to match the bedroom, and use the cross stitch motifs from the patchwork quilt. The two main designs were chosen for the round pot and the heart-shaped trinket pot, and a section of the design suited the small pots perfectly. The cross stitch designs were stitched as above and then fitted into the lids of the pots as instructed by the manufacturer.

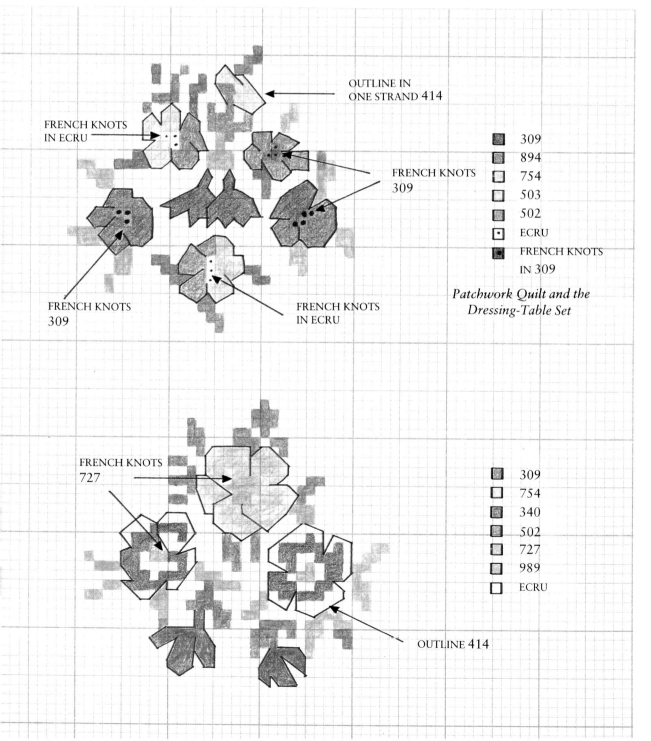

OUTLINE IN ONE STRAND 414

FRENCH KNOTS IN ECRU

FRENCH KNOTS 309

FRENCH KNOTS 309

FRENCH KNOTS IN ECRU

| | |
|---|---|
| ■ | 309 |
| ■ | 894 |
| □ | 754 |
| □ | 503 |
| ■ | 502 |
| · | ECRU |
| ■ | FRENCH KNOTS IN 309 |

*Patchwork Quilt and the Dressing-Table Set*

FRENCH KNOTS 727

| | |
|---|---|
| ■ | 309 |
| □ | 754 |
| ■ | 340 |
| ■ | 502 |
| ■ | 727 |
| □ | 989 |
| □ | ECRU |

OUTLINE 414

# CHAPTER 12

# *Books and Photographs*

This collection of projects is intended to prove just how versatile cross stitch can be. Book covers and picture frames are unusual and make attractive gifts. These hand-decorated mounts can also be used to give old mirrors a new lease of life.

## ORGANISER COVER

There are many loose-leaf organisers and diaries on the market, often at incredible prices. This project uses a cheap model and hides the plastic cover beneath a hand-embroidered sleeve.

*Stitch count:* 50 × 74
*Design size:* 3½ × 5¼in (9 × 13cm)

*MATERIALS (See chart, p112)*
*Aida material in black: 14 blocks to 1in*
*(5 blocks to 1cm)*
*German Flower Threads as listed on the chart*
*Black lining material*
*Purchased organiser file*

To estimate the amount of material needed, measure the file you have purchased. The instructions that follow are for the example illustrated, so you will need to check that the measurements are suitable for your own project.

Cut a piece of material at least 17 × 10in (43 × 25cm) to allow for the design on the front and the pockets on the inside. Fold the fabric in and work a line of tacking threads along the fold. Lay the material face down on a flat surface with the long side towards you. The design will be worked in the right-hand side section of the

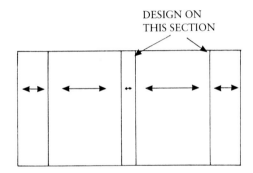

Fig 43 Organiser layout

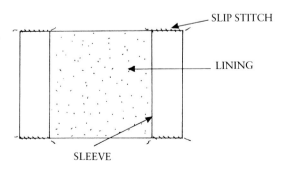

Fig 44 Making up the organiser

material allowing enough margin for the pockets inside.

Stitch the cross stitch design from the chart using one strand of German Flower Thread for the cross stitch. When the design is complete, check for missed stitches and press lightly on the wrong side.

To check the position of the inside sleeves (which will hold the cover in place), wrap the embroidery around the organiser cover and fold the excess inside, checking that the spine will still close properly. When you are satisfied that folds are in the right place, mark with a li of tacking. Now cut a piece of lining material the same size as the Aida and carefully pin to the wrong side, turning in the raw edges as you go. Using small stitches, slip stitch the lining to the Aida with matching threads. Fold the allowance for the sleeve inside on the line of tacking threads and pin in position. Check that the cover will still fit the organiser and then stitch the sides invisibly. Finally, reassemble the transformed organiser.

# ROSE BOOK COVER
# OR GLASSES CASE

This simple design has been taken from an original Berlin pattern and could be used for a glasses case or a book cover.

*Stitch count:* 71 × 31
*Design size:* 5½ × 2½in (14 × 6cm)

MATERIALS *(See chart, p113)*
*Linda fabric: 26 threads to 1in (11 threads to 1cm)*
*Stranded cottons as listed on the chart*
*Polyester wadding as illustrated on the chart*
*Matching lining material*

Cut two pieces of material at least 9 × 6in (23 × 15cm) and one piece 9 × 2½in (23 × 6cm) for the spine. Work the cross stitch design from the chart using two strands of stranded cotton for the cross stitch. When the embroidery is complete, check for missed stitches and press lightly on the wrong side.

The book cover is made up in the same way as the Cottage Diary (p120) Proceed in the same manner, making up each section individually and then joining them all together.

*Organiser Cover, Rose Book Cover or glasses case and family photograph*

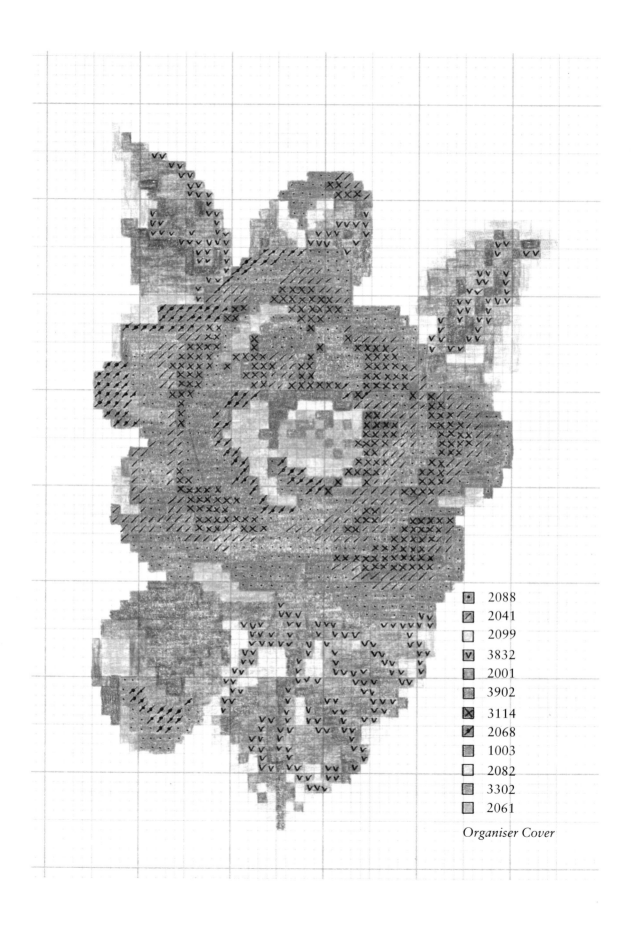

| | |
|---|---|
| ⊡ | 2088 |
| ◪ | 2041 |
| □ | 2099 |
| ☑ | 3832 |
| ◨ | 2001 |
| ▨ | 3902 |
| ⊠ | 3114 |
| ◪ | 2068 |
| ▨ | 1003 |
| □ | 2082 |
| ▨ | 3302 |
| ▨ | 2061 |

*Organiser Cover*

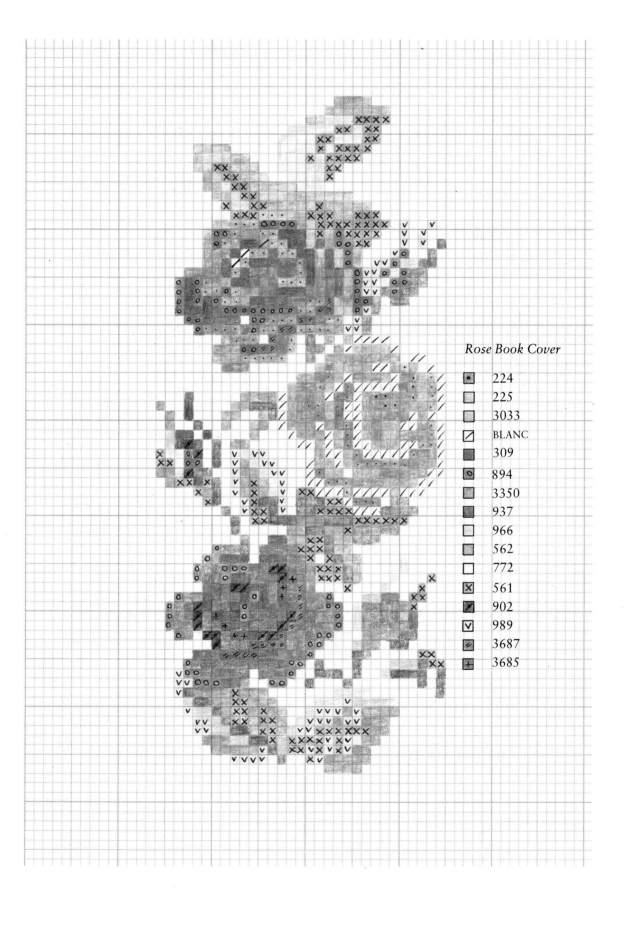

Rose Book Cover

| | |
|---|---|
| ● | 224 |
| □ | 225 |
| □ | 3033 |
| ⧄ | BLANC |
| ■ | 309 |
| ◉ | 894 |
| □ | 3350 |
| ■ | 937 |
| □ | 966 |
| □ | 562 |
| □ | 772 |
| ⊠ | 561 |
| ◩ | 902 |
| Ⅴ | 989 |
| ▨ | 3687 |
| ✚ | 3685 |

# PHOTOGRAPH MOUNTS

All of these mounts are made using the same method. The small square design (p119, chart p118) is stitched in German Flower Thread and the larger pansy mount (chart pp116-17) is stitched in stranded cotton and Marlitt. Both are stitched on unbleached linen, using the charts in this chapter.

The design on the oval mount is from the Roses Evening Bag (p90) and the design on the mount with two photographs (p111) is from the Alphabet Sampler (chart p36).

First, choose a mount to suit the photograph and check that the embroidery you have chosen will fit on the mount – it is very difficult to cut a mount to suit a finished embroidery.

*MATERIALS*
*Fabric to fit chosen mount and photograph*
*Stranded cottons as listed on chosen chart*
*Purchased cardboard mount*
*Double-sided tape*
*Rubber-based adhesive, eg, Copydex*
*Small sharp scissors*

Place the fabric on a clean surface and lay the mount on top, squaring it up with the grain of the fabric. Using tailor's chalk, draw round the outside and inside edges of the mount. Remove the mount. Mark a 2in (5cm) turning allowance on the outside edge and cut the fabric. Do not cut the inside edge – this remains until the embroidery is complete.

Work your chosen embroidery, following the charts and using the suggested threads. When the embroidery is complete, check for missed stitches and press lightly on the wrong side.

Place the mount face up on a clean work surface and place a piece of double-sided tape down one side (this will be removed later). Place the fabric in position over the mount, aligning the embroidery correctly, then press down on the double-sided tape to hold the fabric in position.

Turn the mount and fabric over, check that none of the stitches show through the window – adjust if necessary. Allow a 1in (25mm) turning allowance and cut out the window. Clip the

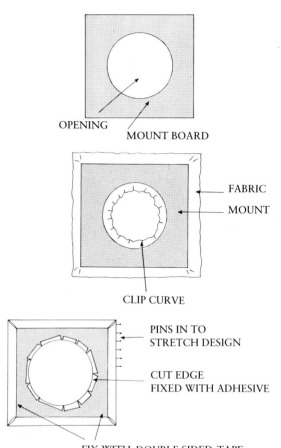

Fig 45 *Making up covered mounts*

curves so that the edge will turn and stick down. Apply a thin coating of adhesive to the inside back edge of the window and stick down the fabric. Leave the mount until the glue is thoroughly dry.

When the glue is dry, remove the double-sided tape carefully and stretch the fabric taut, using pins as shown in the diagram. When the embroidery is stretched, fix the fabric to the back of the mount with double-sided tape.

The mount is then ready for the photograph, which can be fixed in place using double-sided tape. For a professional finish, the photographs can then be framed.

*Pansy Photograph mount*

114

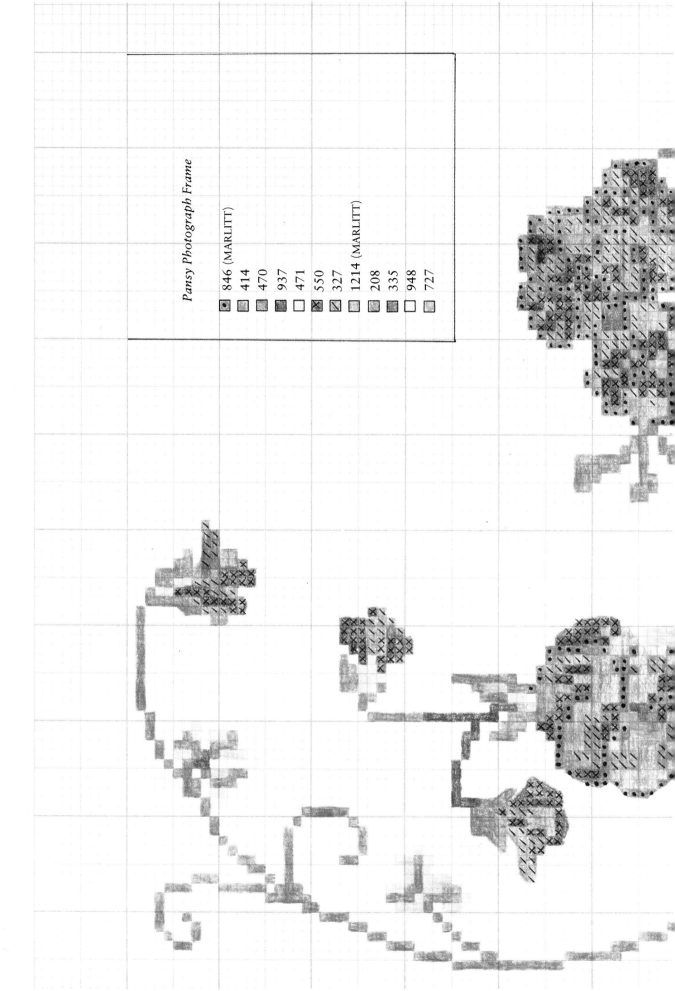

*Pansy Photograph Frame*

- ● 846 (MARLITT)
- ■ 414
- ■ 470
- ■ 937
- □ 471
- ✕ 550
- ◨ 327
- □ 1214 (MARLITT)
- ■ 208
- ■ 335
- □ 948
- □ 727

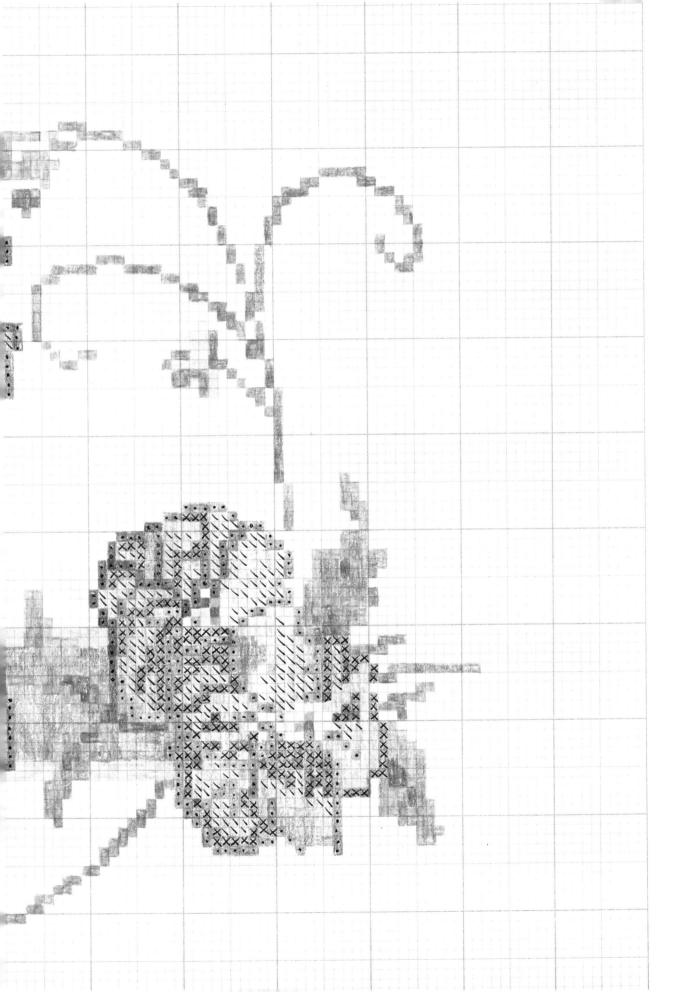

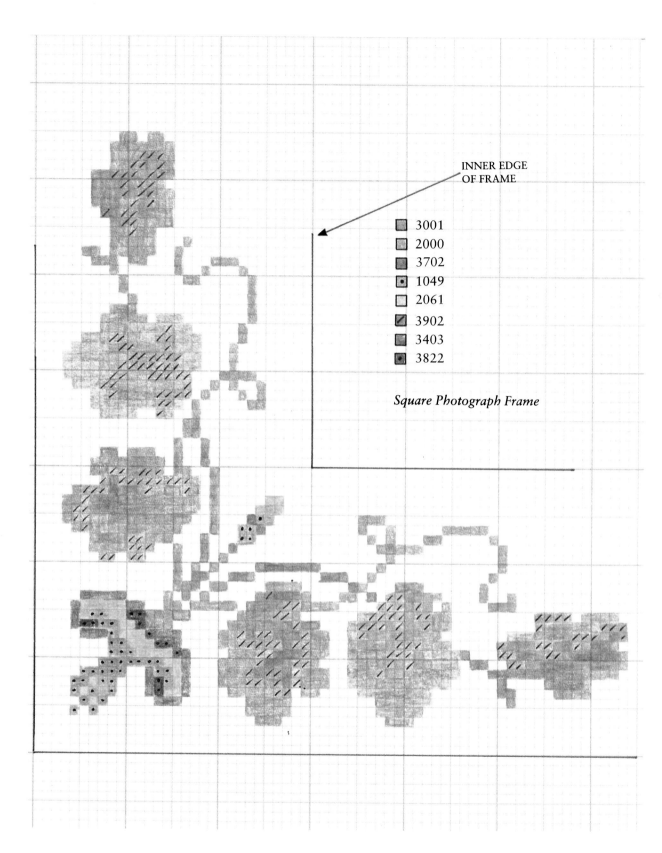

INNER EDGE
OF FRAME

3001
2000
3702
1049
2061
3902
3403
3822

*Square Photograph Frame*

*Greenoff family snaps*

# CHAPTER 13
# Victorian Gardens

These two colourful garden projects derive from the Victorian enthusiasm for all things botanical. The Cottage Diary design was taken from a Victorian postcard found in a junk shop and is stitched in German Flower Thread. The Knot Garden Flower Press uses French knots worked in Designer Silk between the hedges.

## COTTAGE DIARY

The pretty cottage design could also be highly appropriate for a gardener's notebook.

*Stitch count:* 93 × 54
*Design size:* 6½ × 3¾in (16 × 9.5cm)

*MATERIALS (See chart, p122)*
*Linen in natural colour: 28 threads to 1in*
   *(12 threads to 1cm)*

*German Flower Thread as listed on the chart*
*Matching curtain-lining*
*Medium-weight polyester wadding*

   Cut two pieces of linen at least 12 × 10in (30.5 × 25.5cm) for the cover and two pieces at least 2 × 9in (5 × 22.5cm) for the spine
   Take one of the large pieces of linen and set the other pieces aside. Work a narrow hem around

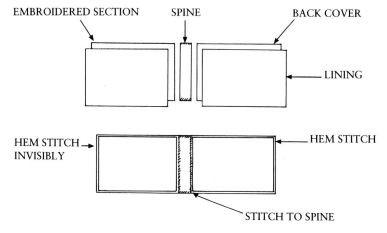

*Fig 46 Making up the cottage diary*

Cottage Diary

*Cottage Diary*

BACK STITCH
IN 1600

| | | |
|---|---|---|
| v 3412 | 1600 | 3312 |

| | | |
|---|---|---|
| 2002 | 2088 | 1001 |
| 3114 | 2068 | 1932 |

| | | |
|---|---|---|
| 3722 | 2061 | 1000 |
| 3403 | 3311 | 2023 |

| | | |
|---|---|---|
| 1500 | 2001 | 3101 |
| 3512 | 3832 | 3732 |

the material to prevent fraying, fold in four and press lightly with a warm iron. Sew a line of tacking threads along the folds to mark the centre. Stitch the cottage design from the chart, starting in the centre of the material. Use one strand of Flower Thread for the cross stitch and the small amount of back stitch outlining.

When the design is complete, check for missed stitches and press lightly on the wrong side.

Carefully measure and cut two pieces of firm card 10 × 8in (25 × 20cm), making sure that they are exactly the same size. Cut two pieces of polyester wadding slightly larger than the card. Cut two pieces of lining fabric 12 × 10in (30.5 × 25.5cm).

The next stage is to make a sort of sandwich of the material and card. Lay your embroidery face down on a clean flat surface and centre a piece of polyester wadding on the top followed by a piece of card. Check that the design is in the right position, fold the linen over the card and lace in position (see diagram). Add the lining by folding in the raw edges and pinning in position. Slip stitch carefully using matching thread. Make the back cover in the same way and set aside until it is needed.

To make the spine, cut a piece of card 10 × 1in (25.5 × 2.5cm) and, using the same method as above, cover the card with the linen. The spine of the example illustrated was entirely enclosed in the linen material, but lining could be used for the inside face if necessary.

Carefully match the edges and stitch the three sections together with strong matching thread.

The diary illustrated has a twisted cord made from co-ordinating coloured thread, the instructions for which are on p94.

# KNOT GARDEN FLOWER PRESS

The press is made up in two sections – the embroidered top and an undecorated base. The base section could be made up from a matching material and does not need to be an even-weave fabric.

*Stitch count:* 80 × 80
*Design size:* 6¼in (15.5cm) square

*MATERIALS (See chart, p126)*
*Linen in ivory: 26 threads to 1in (11 threads to 1cm)*
*Stranded cottons as listed on the chart*
*Designer Silk: cut space-dyed threads as chart*
*Medium-weight polyester wadding*
*Lining material*
*Plywood*
*4 bolts, 4 plain nuts and 4 wing-nuts*

Cut a piece of linen at least 10in (25cm) square and cut a matching piece for the base. Work a narrow hem around the material to prevent fraying, fold into four, press lightly with an iron and mark the folds with a line of tacking threads.

First, sort the yarns. The green hedges are worked in cross stitch using two strands of stranded cotton and are shown on the chart in green crayon. The Algerian eye stitches are also worked in two strands of cotton. All the added colour in the garden is worked in Designer Silk using the space-dyed yarn and in French knots. This silk thread has a range of colours in each length so that when they are worked the French knots are shaded automatically. The idea is to pack lots of French knots into the areas indicated by the colour on the chart. If you cannot use Designer Silk, group together stranded cottons in pinks, purples and yellows, put them on your organiser and pick them at random for a similar effect.

Work the pattern from the chart, starting in the centre, but work the green hedges in cross stitch and the Algerian eye before you start the French knots. When the knot garden begins to take shape, you can pack in the flowers freely without actually counting all the threads.

123

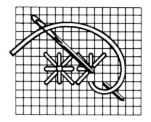

*Fig 47 Algerian eye stitch*

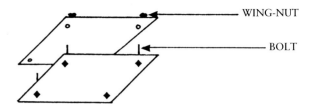

*Fig 49 Making up the flower press*

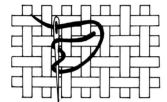

*Fig 48 French knots*

When the embroidery is complete, check for missed stitches and press lightly on the wrong side, taking care not to squash the stitches.

Next, make the press. Cut two pieces of plywood or similar light-weight material to the exact size that the press will be on completion. The example illustrated is 7in (17.5cm) square. Using a drill the correct size for the bolts, make a hole in each corner of the plywood (see chart for position) and repeat this process in the underneath section.

Cut two pieces of polyester wadding and lining material at least 1in (2.5cm) larger than the plywood and set aside.

Using a sharp pair of scissors, make a hole at each corner of the embroidered knot garden (see chart for position) and work a row of button-hole stitch around each opening to prevent fraying. Do the same with the lining fabric.

Lay a piece of plywood on a clean flat surface and cover it with a piece of polyester wadding. Lay the embroidered section on top and carefully fold the excess fabric over the wood and lace in position. Check the position of the stitched design and the four holes, and ease gently if necessary. When you are satisfied with the stretched embroidery, add the lining in the same way as with the diary, but matching the holes on the inside to ensure that the bolts will pass through without damaging the material.

Make up the base of the press in the same way.

For the final assembly, take the plain underneath section and with the right side facing you, pass a bolt through each corner and push firmly home. Turn the press over and fix the bolts in place using the four plain nuts. At this stage you can add sheets of blotting paper and cut sheets of cardboard for the centre of the press. Carefully add the top section, passing the bolts through the material and fixing in position with the wing-nuts.

*Knot Garden Flower Press*

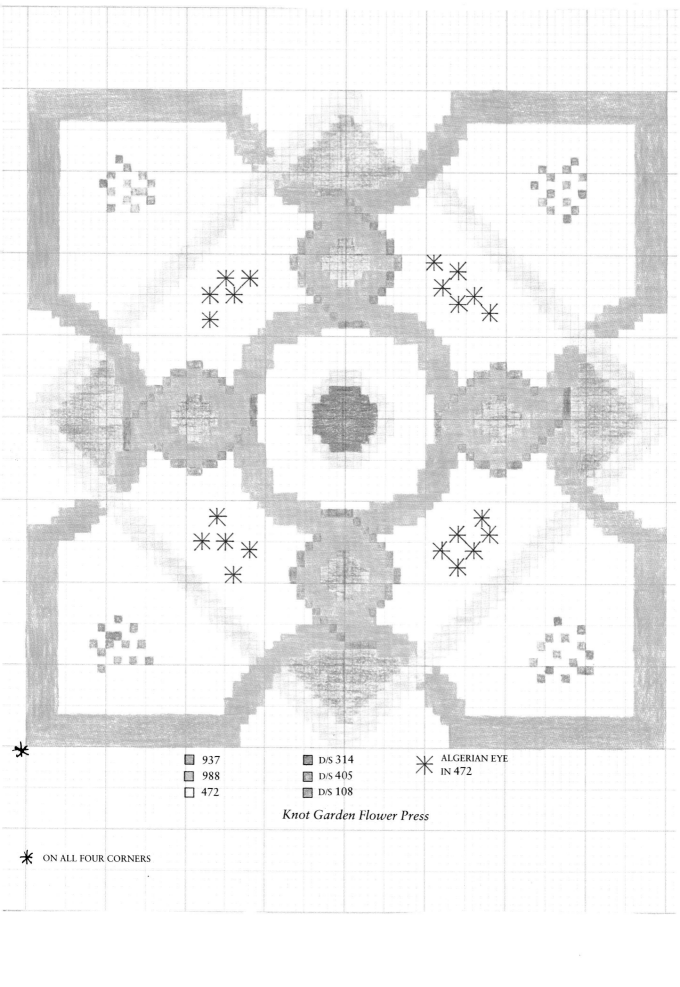

| | 937 | | D/S 314 | ✳ | ALGERIAN EYE |
|---|---|---|---|---|---|
| | 988 | | D/S 405 | | IN 472 |
| | 472 | | D/S 108 | | |

*Knot Garden Flower Press*

✳ ON ALL FOUR CORNERS

# ACKNOWLEDGEMENTS

I would like to thank the following people for the help and support I have received whilst writing this book.

Michel Standley, who continued to run The Inglestone Collection in my absence, and whose hard work and loyalty is much appreciated. The rest of the Inglestone team, Jean, Daphne, Thelma, Rita, Liz and Diane who have kept things running so smoothly, plus all the staff and trainees at Newholme Day Centre and The Adult Opportunity Centre, Cirencester.

All the enthusiastic stitchers who made the book possible: Dorothy Presley, Angie Davidson, Hanne Castelo, Di Fallows, Elizabeth Lydan, Vera Greenoff and Ruth Mowat.

My dear friend, Ursula Joka-Deubelius whose enthusiasm is such an inspiration and Rosalind Parnell who introduced us. Stanley Duller who first introduced me to Berlin charts and has taught me so much. Isabel Elliott for her valuable practical help when I most needed it. Sarah-Jane Gillespie for her miniature pen and ink sketches. Lesley O'Brien for her special watercolour painting in the introductory chapter. Jean McLaughlin for my china hearts and encouragement. Di Lewis for her lovely photography.

I would also like to thank the following companies and organisations for advice and supplies used in the book: The Embroiderers Guild, Hampton Court; The Natural History Museum, London for permission to use the material from the Botany Library; Yardley of London for permission to use *The Cries of London* etching as inspiration; Tunleys and Son, Fleet St, Swindon, for art and framing supplies; Framecraft Miniatures Ltd, Birmingham for trays, trinket pots and jewellery; MacGregor Designs, Burton on Trent for the wooden pincushion base; Campden Needlecraft Centre, Chipping Campden, Glos; Voirrey Embroidery, Brimstage, Wirral; The Ladies Work Society, Moreton in Marsh, Glos; DMC Creative World, Pullman Road, Leicester; Liberty of London for the Liberty lawn used for the bed cover. Sue Mason of Flower Studio, Lechlade.

The miniature chest of drawers is available from Voirrey Embroidery. The sweetheart cushions were made by Jill Miles and are available from Hepatica, Wilmslow, Cheshire. The Victorian Doll was made by Gillie Charlson of Anderton, Chorley, Lancs; loaned and dressed by Joan Nerini, 54, Mulgrave Road, Ealing, London (whose patterns are available by mail order).

When writing to any of the suppliers listed, please enclose a SAE for your reply.

More information about The Inglestone Collection can be obtained from: The Inglestone Collection, Milton Place, Fairford Glos, GL7 4HR, telephone (0285) 712778 (enclose SAE when writing).

# BIBLIOGRAPHY

*The New Anchor Book of Counted Thread Embroidery Stitches* [David & Charles]

*Linen Stitches* Ginnie Thompson [Ginnie Thompson Guild, 1987]

*Flowercraft* Violet Stevenson [Hamlyn, 1977]

*Victorian People* Asa Briggs [Penguin, 1945]

*Picture it in Cross stitch* Jo Verso [David & Charles, 1988]

*Victorian Canvas Work* Molly Proctor [Batsford, 1972]

*A Victorian Posy* (ed) Sheila Pickles [Penhaligons, 1987]

*The Subversive Stitch* Rozsika Parker [The Women's Press, 1984]

# INDEX